NAKED MA

NAKED MARKETING

*How the 4Ps have destroyed business
and what to do about it*

Sue Nelson

2000

First published in 2010 by Management Books 2000 Ltd
Forge House, Limes Road
Kemble, Cirencester
Gloucestershire, GL7 6AD, UK
Tel: 0044 (0) 1285 771441
Fax: 0044 (0) 1285 771055
Email: info@mb2000.com
Web: www.mb2000.com

British Library Cataloguing in Publication Data is available

ISBN 9781852526351

CONTENTS

2. WHAT TO DO INSTEAD

3. DO YOU KNOW YOUR CUSTOMERS?

4. CAN YOU SOLVE THEIR PROBLEMS?

5. HAVE THEY HEARD OF YOU?

6. WHERE CAN THEY FIND OUT MORE?

7. HOW DO YOU COMPARE TO THE COMPETITION?

8. WHAT ARE YOU LIKE TO DEAL WITH?

9. A NEW DEFINITION FOR A NEW WORLD

10. SOME PREDICTIONS

PREFACE

You've read the book, now get the t-shirt

The Four Ps is a dusty old marketing roadmap unfit for a new century. Everyone knows it has passed its *sell by* date. We can all complain that it doesn't fit anymore, but someone has to replace it with a model that embraces advances in technology, our different attitude to authority, capitalism and consumerism, and the hard reality of organisational survival. This book offers an alternative to the Four Ps, at last. It is relatively jargon-free and proves that basing today's marketing strategy around a theory dreamt up in the 1960s, is at best, foolhardy. This book is the marketing equivalent of the 'Emperor's New Clothes', with everything stripped away, and marketing mythologies laid bare. That's why it's called *Naked Marketing*.

There are hundreds of books on every marketing subject from branding to advertising, public relations to distribution. Many are business and management texts of the 'inspirational' style. However, even if you accept the arguments or hypotheses proffered, they don't always give the step-by-step guide or hints as to what your next move might be. They're inspiring, of course, but what do you actually do after you've read them? Some are aimed purely at consumer marketing, others for service marketing, few for social or public campaigning. They tend to assume that your company has a turnover of £100 million a year, and you have a massive marketing budget. But of the 4.7 million businesses in the UK, 4.6 million employ less than fifty people, so most of us are just not in that bracket.

Other marketing books are intense academic tomes, aimed at top executives who have to construct hugely complicated international marketing strategies, or students on marketing-related courses. But day-to-day commercial marketing isn't actually that difficult. It's common sense, and the end point, or key measurement, is not about awareness or creating buzz – it's about people buying your product, service or message. If they don't buy it, you've wasted your marketing money and you might as well not bother.

Marketing is therefore a straight investment decision – if you invest (say) a marketing budget of £25,000 and if you don't get at least £25,750 (3%) in increased sales back (not total sales, *increased sales*), you should have stuck the money in a bank propped up by the government instead.

So this book doesn't give a detailed academic viewpoint of marketing, nor does it assume you work in a multi-million pound company with an advertising budget to match. It will give you an initial overview of marketing, how it fits together as an overall process, and as you get more experienced or confident, you can find those other texts and books, which will give you more technical detail if you need it.

But the key to the success of any business book, is not whether you are enthused with the methodology or inspirational thrust, it's whether you will do anything with it. When I read such books or arrive back from some training or a conference, I feel inspired and pledge to take a new approach, but then I get back to work and gradually fall into old habits and routines.

What is really difficult, is translating all the information you were so inspired by, into positive action. This book not only explains a new marketing methodology, but gives you guidance on where to get help, by outlining the choices you have, regardless of budget. You can put each of the six elements of Isaiah Logic into action tomorrow. So this book, is not where you just read and agree (or not) with the assertions made, it's where you need to take action and do something about your organisation to reach the objectives and targets you have set yourself.

In a challenging climate the alternatives are not attractive or promising. So, as the Nike advertising goes – *just do it*.

A note on social and cause related marketing

Social marketing is a term increasingly being used to describe the achievement and sustainability of certain behaviours relevant to a range of social issues and topics. There is a fairly well accepted definition articulated by Dr Jeff French (Director) and Clive Blair-Stevens (Deputy Director) of the National Social Marketing (NSM) Centre:

> *"the systematic application of marketing alongside other concepts and techniques, to achieve specific behavioural goals, for a social or public good."*[1]

Social marketing's primary aim therefore is to achieve a particular 'social good' (rather than commercial benefit) with specific behavioural goals clearly identified and targeted. It's the marketing of a message that intends to elicit a reaction that eventually results in behaviour change, or initiates a certain behaviour. Examples include campaigning on health issues such as stopping smoking, or on social issues such as dropping litter. Cause-related marketing also attempts to deliver a behavioural response, but tends to have an outcome that leads to the support (financial or otherwise) of a particular cause, such as nuclear disarmament, cancer research or a political party.

The NSM Centre website[2] is a useful source of information on social marketing, as is the Institute for Social Marketing's site[3], but both are preoccupied with health. Obviously this is a huge part of social campaigning, but not its entirety. Whilst we may remember the 1950's "coughs and sneezes spread diseases" message, and we know we drink and eat too much, social marketing encompasses behaviour change in a very wide area from graffiti, knife crime, drink driving, volunteering, recycling and so on.

The NSM Centre also aims to articulate a marketing process that is specific to social marketing. As they have rightly observed, the

---

[1] French, Blair-Stevens 2006
[2] www.nsmc.org.uk
[3] The Institute of Social Marketing is based at the University of Stirling, and can be found at www.ism.stir.ac.uk

Four Ps are a hopeless model for achieving behaviour change. However, the Isaiah Logic process is just as applicable to social and cause-related marketing as product and service marketing, and indeed I've used this model in a charity campaigning for behaviour change for many years, with spectacular audited results. If a marketing model is right, which I believe Isaiah Logic is, it doesn't need to be adapted for different branches of marketing; all the constituent parts make sense no matter what your marketing aim. The skill in using Isaiah Logic is making marketing choices in each of the elements of the process, including deciding which parts are more important or require more emphasis than others.

If you are involved in social or cause related marketing, I believe this book is as useful to you as it is to someone in the private sector (for a change!).

PART 1

HOW TO DESTROY YOUR BUSINESS IN FOUR EASY STEPS

FOUR PS INTRODUCTION

The Cilla Black of marketing strategy

When someone mentions the four Ps, I immediately know they have no idea at all about marketing in the 21st Century. It's the Cilla Black of marketing strategy – no matter how you try to dress it up, it has a strong whiff of the last century about it.

If you base your organisation's marketing on the four Ps, it means you don't really have a customer-centric philosophy and you do your marketing upside down and back to front. You get customers by luck not judgment and you're seriously out of touch. Like Cilla, it served us well for a couple of decades, and we have an inexplicable affection for it, but it really is time to move on. The frivolous times are over and the competitive climate is much tougher.

The four Ps are the individual elements of a total package that makes up the so-called "marketing mix", as coined by Neil Borden[4] who first started using the phrase in 1949:

"When building a marketing program to fit the needs of his firm, the marketing manager has to weigh the behavioural forces and then juggle marketing elements in his mix with a keen eye on the resources with which he has to work."

They didn't have women in those days.

The most common variables used in constructing a marketing mix were outlined by Jerome McCarthy[5]. He called them the four Ps, and essentially developed a marketing methodology that viewed the world from a marketer's perspective. It stands for *Product,*

---

[4] Borden, N. (1964) "The concept of the marketing mix" Journal of Advertising Research, vol 4, June 1964.
[5] McCarthy, J. (1960 1st ed.), Basic Marketing: A managerial approach, (13th ed. 2001)

Price, Promotion and *Place.* In more detail they more or less represent the following[6]:

Product

- Product production
- Product range, breadth, depth and mix
- Product features and quality
- Packaging

Price

- Price levels, discounts, pricing strategies
- Credit policy

Promotion

- Advertising; spend, copy, content, media selection and scheduling
- Sales promotion and personal selling
- Other forms of publicity

Place

- Channels of distribution
- Stock levels and delivery

You only need concentrate on these four in sequence, and your product or service will fly off the shelf. The basic elements of the theory have been around for fifty years with periodic refinements, but generally it's supposed to be a step-by-step framework which acts as a guideline to implement a marketing strategy. According to Kotler et al[7] the mix is a set of:

"controllable tactical marketing tools... that the firm blends to produce the response it wants in the target market."

---

[6] As elaborated on by Lancaster, G. and Massingham, L. (1993), *Essentials of Marketing: Text and Cases.*

[7] Kotler, P., Armstrong, G., Saunders, J., and Wong, V. (1999), *Principles of Marketing (2nd European ed.)*

No mention of the customer in all that, and thereby hangs the problem. The theory is based on the premise that marketers, or their organisations, are in control; that the customer is somehow the end point, and an unwitting and naïve pawn in the complex tactical game of getting them to part with their money, use your service or agree with your message. Apparently if you get "the mix" right, customers will miraculously beat a path to your door. Yeah, right, not any more.

In effect it's a supply side model that pushes out towards the customer, with the assumption that there isn't a context of over-supply or liquidity problems and that lots of people unquestionably want your product or service offering. This scenario just doesn't sound like the fight for potential customers that most organisations find themselves in, year after year. But educators and academics used to quite like the concept, because it's reasonably simplistic and easy to teach, and it instinctively rings true. If, that is, you live in a parallel universe where customers do exactly as their told, which they may well have done back in 1960.

Its slow agonising demise was prolonged in the 1980s when Porter[8] legitimised the concept, by pointing out that this gave the marketer the opportunity to add value to each part of the mix. It gave marketing a professional credibility and status within the supplying organisation. We were no longer the inscrutable and unaccountable masters of the fuzzy art of getting sales, we had a real profession. One that, supposedly, had a scientific model from Harvard at its heart. Alas, however it started from the viewpoint that the marketer, not the customer, had the power of control over purchases, and it further enforced the emphasis on the supply chain approach.

The foie gras panacea

Although the theory has been the de facto methodological marketing process for a couple of generations, it hasn't been without its critics, some of whom argued that "it oversimplifies the

---

[8] Porter, M.E., (1985), *Competitive Advantage: Creating and Sustaining Superior Performance.*

reality of marketing management"[9]. By 1990 Robert Lauterborn[10] hit on something by saying that each of these variables should also be seen from a consumer's perspective. Quite right. But instead of being brave and dishing the dirt on the old fashioned concept, he tried to evolve the concept by converting *Product* into "customer solution", *Price* into "cost to the customer", *Place* into "convenience", and *Promotion* into "communication". He called these the four Cs, thus accidentally cementing the 'four' legitimacy still further.

But increasingly you could tell it didn't reflect the real world, which is why theorisers try to play around with the model, retro-fitting it into modern reality. None of us has devoted the time, or was confident or radical enough, to properly predict the future with some insight and imagination. We should have ditched it and just started from scratch but the four Ps entered into the collective marketing mindset, and it's very hard to shift.

In the 1990's instead of us bravely stating that the four Cs and four Ps were plainly irrelevant, an extra three Ps were shoved down our throats when we weren't looking. Booms and Bitner[11] rather unhelpfully perpetuated the P thing, by adding *People*, *Process* and *Physical Evidence*. I even heard that there were some moves to add *Partnership* to it, in order to reflect the "growing focus in marketing toward long-term orientation". God help us all.

So despite the occasional sideline comment, the theory has been force-fed to all professional (and wannabe) marketers and ended up being the foie gras panacea for bottom-line success. But for most organisations to follow this premise today is at worst a threat to their business, and at best a waste of marketing money. The process is fatally flawed and the age of the credit crunch demands something more practical, logical and helpful, not just to business owners, but those in the public and third sectors.

---

[9] Jobber, D. (1998), *Principles and Practice of Marketing* (2nd ed.).
[10] Lauterborn, R (1990) "New Marketing Litany: 4P's Passe; C words take over", *Advertising Age*, Oct 1990
[11] Booms, B. H. and Bitner, M-J. (1981), "Marketing Strategies and Organisation Structures for Service Firms", in *Marketing of Services*, J. H. Donnelly and W. R. George, Eds.

PRODUCT

The top banana?

Before proposing a new practical marketing model, it's important to see why the four Ps are so harmful as a concept in the 21st century. To begin with nowadays the choice of products, lifestyle choices and even educational options is almost overwhelming. When I go to my local supermarket for some orange juice, it's not an easy decision. The Tropicana brand alone has eight different types, if you don't count the 'smoothie' option that is. And while I ponder over which one I prefer, I'm surrounded by 40,000 other products that I could buy between there and the checkout. In the UK, I can apparently take my pick of dozens of types of dental floss, more than 400 brands of shampoo, 600 kinds of coffee and 2,000 different types of car[12]. It's a choice explosion, and depending on the amount of money involved, I need a good deal of information if I have any chance of making an informed buying decision. The choice of services I can use is just as diverse and daunting, as is the plethora of businesses that offer them. How and why, do I choose one product or service over another?

From the days when we were fooled into thinking flared trousers were fashionable, we have steadily been over-producing goods. We have churned out more and more products at a rate that we cannot buy and use them. The serious downturn in the high street is part of this pattern, and I cannot see why economists keep scratching their heads over disappointing retail figures. It seems blindingly obvious to me – we produce or import more products than we can use so we've reached a peak of consumption, and when I'm strapped for cash I get serious about what I buy. The apparent rise in our population from immigrant workers may give us some growth, but in general are they big spenders?

---

[12] The Future Foundation, (2000)

As I get older and generally become more affluent I won't buy more stuff, but I might well replace what I have with a more expensive model or with something completely different that serves the same function. When I want to upgrade, or something is on the blink or completely broken, I'll go on a bit of a shopping spree, but basically our family is all stocked up thanks and just now I'm not going to buy something for the sake of it. I'm sure we're not the only ones. This isn't the 1960s where consumerism was somewhat new and products were in demand. OK, what we have might not be the most expensive, or the best design, or great quality, but we do have everything we need. So I'm not going to buy more than one car, microwave, settee, mobile phone, cooker or vacuum cleaner. I only need two loaves of Hovis a week, so no matter how good the advertising, I'm not going to buy more. I might upgrade or buy an alternative, but I won't buy more.

The point is, people are now used to overwhelming choice, they know there's a fight for their money or their custom and they're in the driving seat, especially now. With such a range of choices they're used to being in control, even pre-teens are taught to discriminate and use their power as consumers as soon as they have a bit of discretion over their pocket money. So, no matter what type of customer, or what age, none of them will put up with mediocre service, shoddy goods, so-so entertainment or disappointing hospitality experiences.

Kotler and McCarthy argued that *product* was the starting point for developing and implementing marketing strategy:

"Anything that can be offered to a market for attention, acquisition, use or consumption that might satisfy a want or need. It includes physical objects, services, persons, places, organisations and ideas."

But nowadays that's simply not true. In an environment of increasing unemployment, over-production and over-provision, the assertion that the product is the beginning of the process, and we can just churn it out, and flog it to an unsuspecting consumer who *might* want it, is absurd.

It's no different for service industries. You could be the world's best company for typewriter sales and servicing. As a marketer I could put loads of budget and effort into promoting the business and follow the sequential rules set out by the four Ps, but it's fairly obvious you wouldn't get one customer. No-one uses typewriters anymore. I don't think my seventeen year old daughter could even describe what one looks like. You simply cannot start with any old product or any service, and expect a marketing department to flog it and get results.

Perhaps you could argue then, that competitive edge can be gained not by selling an existing service or product, but by service or product innovation, hence the product does come first after all. But that doesn't make sense either because you need to talk to people before you start developing, otherwise how do you know if anyone wants it? In most cases you need to develop new products or service innovations that predict customer needs and you cannot do it in the rarified air of a laboratory, wearing a white lab coat cut off from the outside world, so it cannot, and must not, be the marketing starting point either.

In fairness, beginning with the product was probably developed in a context where there was less competition, and where the consumer had far less choice i.e. where customers felt they were lucky to get their hands on a product, and there weren't that many buying choices, but clearly that's not the case today.

So, if most of us have more or less everything we need and there are endless choices concerning the products we buy, services we choose, lifestyle we want to lead and so on, when we do make purchasing decisions the power rests with us, the customer, not the provider or producer. To craft a thorough sales or marketing strategy using the product development function as top banana, would put the customer at the end of the process not the beginning yet again. We need to start with our customers.[13]

---

[13] When developing products, it's important not to immediately dismiss ideas because of barriers to production. Take Kozo Ohsone, the then General Manager of Sony's tape recorder business division. He encouraged his staff to try their ideas before they had time to think about the difficulties that might arise. Famously, the Walkman was born in this way, with Ohsone managing his team so that they overcame all hurdles to eventually turn the idea into a commercially viable product.

DON'T TRY THIS AT HOME

Marketing disasters – product

Rover – give that dog a bone

All cars are global products. They literally have components from every country around the world. Car making? There's no such thing really, it's not manufacturing, it's assembly. Like a mega meccano kit, but presumably with the instructions in 48 different languages. Cars don't just share little bits like wiring, CD players or windscreen wipers. They share big bits too like the same platform or engine. That's how the economics work. Scratch a Jaguar and hey presto it's a Mondeo underneath. A Skoda? No longer a skip with wheels but a Volkswagen with a lower status badge, but increasing in credibility.

It's fairly obvious then that underneath the bonnet and seats, cars in defined price brackets have huge similarities. So if they're largely the same, the key to sales must be differentiation on the stuff you can see, real innovation on the look and feel of the car, and the development of a brand which buyers will covet. A classic marketing business in fact, where innovation, design and desirability will get the sale.

So when BMW put the Rover Group up for sale in March 2000, minus of course the Mini, the new owners decided they would go down the four P's 'product' route. They also decided not to make any real investments in marketing, innovation or design, and used the "undercut your rivals" pricing policy too. There's a downside in using cheapness as a long term differentiator however, because it involves severely cutting costs, and that means you can't pay for development and innovation – an ever decreasing downward spiral. To be honest it's usually a short term tactic to gain market share or a strategy used for 'commodity' products, but they decided to use it for the long term in an industry where perceived innovation is critical and where cars get a makeover every four years or so. Instead, they fell into production-led madness, the same strategy that destroyed the rest of the British car-making industry a few decades ago.

Unbelievably the new Rover owners, that bought the company for a tenner from BMW (that should've given them a hint), declared their strategy was to "keep the cars as they were". Pile 'em high and sell 'em cheap. You can imagine it in the factory canteen: "Don't worry lads, Rover is British and people are loyal. They're not swayed by flashy foreign rubbish."

Any marketing professional will tell you that consumers aren't loyal to anything much anymore, and it's certainly not a good idea to bet thousands of jobs on the fact that they are. There are many examples in British manufacturing, where the management and workforce forgot the world around them, worked hard and got absorbed in their craftsmanship turning out machines and goods that were a direct result of the production process in the factory. But when they looked up their traditional buyers had been unfaithful and traded in the old battleaxe for a younger, sexier model, and they didn't come back. Ironic that the Japanese motorcycle industry, thrived as a result of British kamikaze tactics. The well-documented perils of product-led business philosophies are plainly evident and yet many marketers are still taught the four P's with the Product being first. Why?

Meanwhile how did the German BMW company, market the new Mini? They carefully crafted and highlighted its 'Britishness', allowing the buyer to infinitely customise their own car. If that's not humiliating enough, you can even order one with a Union Jack plastered on the roof. Rover's competitive counter-attack at the time? Any colour so long as it's old fashioned. Yet more breathtaking irony.

PRICE

The Madonna principle

Comparatively, there's more money floating about than ever before, even in a credit crunch. In real terms people have three times the amount of disposable income than they did in 1960[14]. So we should be able to charge premium prices for most things because people can afford it. Wrong.

Setting the right price is the second element of the four Ps, but nowadays it's all so much more complicated. People can compare our product or service with the competition in an instant, not just in the UK but with overseas competitors too. Even the same product, say a Prada handbag, can be sold for vastly different sums depending on whether you wish to obtain it from Selfridges, a cut-price designer outlet, e-bay or shipped over from South East Asia. Again, the customer has the power, because they have infinite choice *and* access to knowledge. They can make almost instant, detailed comparisons, so it's really quite difficult to make premium pricing stick.

Truly innovative new products or services initially don't have any competition, they are really the only ones that can guarantee a high price. Product or service innovation is a foundation of competitive advantage and a key element of business success[15] – even more so as we enter the beginnings of a post-capitalist, knowledge-based society, where constant change and fluctuations produce new situations and opportunities. It's the age of "hyper-competition"[16].

The unending and increasing stream of knowledge, and the fact that UK consumers, not to mention the media, are novelty mad and fickle with it, means we have to focus even harder on being

---

[14] Source: OECD 2002/nVision and "Economic Trends" Office of National Statistics
[15] E.g. see Nonaka and Takeuchi, (1995).
[16] D'Aveni, (1994)

innovative. Like Madonna we just have to keep re-inventing ourselves. But the advantage of novelty is short-lived. As soon as you launch, in an instant your competitors will have analysed your service business model or stripped down your product, and will be looking to replicate it, only cheaper.

You could try to come up with a scientific pricing model, but even that's practically impossible. Consumers can pay peanuts for some things but be totally extravagant on others. One day I can pay £4 for a single cup of coffee at Starbucks, and on another day pay the same amount to buy a burger each for a family of four at McDonalds. I could do all this whilst wearing a £200 pair of designer trainers, a £20 fake Rolex from Hong Kong, a £2 t-shirt from Primark and some free sample perfume from the page of a magazine. The public are totally inconsistent in their attitude to pricing even during financially hard times.

Buyers are also used to paying for things in many different ways – you can agree leasing, hire purchase or interest-free credit agreements with them, or they might want to use bank transfers, bankers drafts, instant money transfers, personal cheques, credit cards, debit cards or PayPal payment methods, not to mention the (almost extinct) use of cash.

The service industry particularly, has gained from offering propositions that save valuable minutes, hours or even days – dog walking, oven cleaning, take away food, courier services, video conferencing, etc. Again the problem with the four Ps methodology is it does not adequately address the issue of customers that are strapped, not always for cash, but for time. Nor does it address the influence of different payment methods and their inconsistent attitude towards pricing policies.

Pricing can be dramatically affected by a range of issues, but there's only really one pricing tactic, and maybe there always has been: Use the payment method that customers find quick and easy, and if the product or service is more or less the same as everyone else's you have to price match the competition, you're forced to enter into price competition, i.e. be cheaper than your competitors. If you're not in that situation you should charge as much as customers will let you get away with, as long as they *perceive* it's worth it. Any way you look at it, you need to start with the customer and work out what they can afford, and compare that to your competitors' pricing models.

DON'T TRY THIS AT HOME

Marketing disasters – pricing

Coca-Cola – "Dasani"

It seems unbelievable when you can get a glass of water out of the tap at home or work, but bottled water has been a steadily growing marketing in the UK, even though the quality of our drinking water is more than adequate. The bottled water market is the world's fastest growing beverage category at $40 billion sales a year, with the UK market alone worth nearly £2 billion annually, and growing rapidly[17].

Coca-Cola's worldwide bottled water sales have increased by 50% over the last few years and its non-cola sales account for 36% of its revenues. So a move into 'purified' bottle water in the UK, as opposed to natural spring water, was probably inevitable especially as the purified versions account for just under half the world's bottled water sales. Apparently observers in the US say that Americans value 'processing' whilst Europeans value 'naturalness'. But does the British public understand the difference between natural and purified water?

Even though Coca-Cola owns the Malvern natural spring water brand, they decided that they should launch 'Dasani' as a purified water in the UK. It had been a runaway success in the US, with sales of $765 million. It has also performed well

---

[17] According to Market Research company, Zenith International, in 2004

in more than twenty countries, particularly in Latin America and Asia. But if Europeans don't really value processing of water, should they call it 'purified' or some other descriptor, and what about the pricing tactic – surely if it's not natural, but only purified, it should have a much lower price?

Coca-Cola executives agreed a £7 million budget for the UK marketing push, and decided that instead of labelling it 'purified' they would call it 'pure'. In the rest of Europe they agreed to use natural water as their base, but in the UK they would use tap water as it was pretty good already. A selling price of 95p per half litre would strengthen its claim as a relatively upmarket brand, and add weight to its 'pure' credentials, rather than purified. They used water supplied by Thames Water from the tap in their factory in Sidcup, Kent adding a batch of calcium chloride, containing bromide, pumping ozone through it, to give it a better "taste profile".

To justify the premium pricing, Coca-Cola's advertising and marketing claimed it had used a "highly sophisticated purification process" based on Nasa spacecraft technology, which was in fact reverse osmosis used in many modest domestic water purification units. Their mark-up was 0.03p to 95p per half litre. Given that factory staff knew the bottled water was actually Thames Water which they could drink out of the tap at home, it wasn't long before the press got hold of the story. Coca-Cola may have ridden out the media storm if their pricing strategy hadn't aimed for the premium end, but all it did was increase the feeling that the public had been conned. Sales dipped dramatically.

Not long after, it was revealed that the water contained unsafe levels of a potentially carcinogenic agent. By pumping ozone through safe drinking water they were oxidising the bromide, which resulted in a standard Dasani bottle containing twice the legal limit for bromate, which was considered a small but unacceptable cancer-inducing risk by The Drinking Water Inspectorate. Dasani was now considered not only ridiculously over-priced but an unsafe drinking water, and was immediately withdrawn from supermarket shelves in the UK. It has never reappeared.

An executive from a beverage rival told the *The Sunday Times*, "It's typical Coke arrogance. They assume they can replicate what they have done in the US. Well, they can't." Author of *Pop: Truth and Power at the Coca-Cola Company*, Constance Hays, stated:

"The Dasani crisis is a case of a giant that is so desperate for growth that it appears things are being overlooked. Coke is a master marketer—they can sell pretty much anything—but sometimes they get so caught up in the marketing they lose touch with reality."

People don't mind paying a premium if there is real added value, with honest claims to differentiation and quality. However, Dasani has been a public relations disaster for the world's biggest soft-drink manufacturer, revealing a readiness to deceive for the sake of high prices with huge margins.

PROMOTION

Aeronautical engineering to pigeon fancying

When I began my marketing career in London in the mid-1980s, the remit pretty much fell into two halves: *above-the-line*, which broadly meant television and radio advertising, and *below-the-line*, which was printed media in the form of sales literature and adverts in the press. It was therefore straightforward when advising a client. You just absorbed the product research and learnt how to be an art director for the broadcast stuff, and made sure you developed a comprehensive brief and employed good graphic designers, photographers and copywriters for printed advertising.

The ability to understand the main mediums and then make channel decisions wasn't too difficult. After all at the time, there were only two television stations that carried advertising, and Channel 4 was just a couple of years old, so big media spend meant ITV. Since then, with the advent of satellite and cable, the number of television channels has risen dramatically. In the last decade alone it has gone from 56 to 271[18]. Which one to choose for my tv ad?

Around the mid 1980s, radio in Britain simply consisted of state-owned BBC radio and privately owned commercial radio regulated by the IBA[19]. In terms of audience figures, advertising on Capital Radio was rumoured to be the only decent option, unless you had a whacky client who was happy to go for an ad on Radio Caroline (Ahoy there!). By 1994 there were 218 radio stations, and by 2004 that had risen to 455.[20]

Whilst national daily newspapers are largely the same in number, regional, trade and lifestyle magazines have considerably

[18] The Communications Market 2004, Ofcom (2005)
[19] Independent Broadcast Authority
[20] The Communications Market 2004, Ofcom (2005)

increased. Literally thousands are available on every subject imaginable from aeronautical engineering to pigeon fancying. Back then the popular myth was that all magazines were dwarfed in circulation terms, by two main titles. There certainly weren't any men's magazines and the daringly blatant nature of FHM was unthinkable. But if you wanted to get to a female audience, it was Radio Times or Woman's Own. I kid you not.

Recent, media fragmentation makes it incredibly difficult to decide where to appear. It has exploded into a million tiny pieces. If the definition of *Promotion* remains[21], then the only chance of getting this communication dilemma solved is to work out where your customers already spend their media viewing time. If archetypal grandads were one of your target audiences, you couldn't get them to habitually watch your advert on MTV. So you have to work out what they do watch, hear or visit and make sure that's where you are, (promotionally speaking).

You could go for a scatter gun approach and spend thousands on a slot in the middle of Coronation Street, hoping to catch your target market in amongst there somewhere, but most of us don't have the type of budget that can run a sustained campaign that will truly hit the collective consciousness by pure repetition. An advertising 'spot' can range from over one minute to seven seconds, the cost of using such 'spots' varies according to the time of day, the number of homes in the region in which it is broadcast, and audience viewing figures for the programme. A thirty second weekday spot during peak time in London will cost in the region of £20,000. Companies can also sponsor programmes themselves, Cadburys spent £10 million a year when they were sponsoring Coronation Street, appearing at the beginning and close of each section of the programme. But is it worth the money?

Many people don't watch adverts, preferring instead to pop to the toilet, make a cup of tea, or increasingly, if it has been pre-recorded, fast forward to the next bit of the programme. Anyhow if it's teenagers you're after, they're notoriously the lowest

---

[21] "activities that communicate the product or service and its merits to target customers and persuade them to buy."

participants in all the traditional media channels. Working out the ways in which your target audience accesses information and how you can exploit that, is far more efficient and effective than spending millions on tv advertising, but it takes more brain power and planning.

DON'T TRY THIS AT HOME

Marketing disasters – promotion

Egg – "guinea pigs"

A television campaign particularly aimed at parents was launched to increase take up of the Egg Credit Card. Developed by Mother advertising agency, the campaign aimed to engage and educate customers on the benefits of the card and reinforce the caring, open and honest nature of the Egg brand. The proposition, was that the card was so revolutionary Egg tested it on guinea pigs before giving it to consumers, (groundbreaking eh?).

The advert was filmed using actors wearing specially constructed guinea pig body suits with custom-made clothes. They were trained and choreographed by an expert in animal movement, to give them the correct body articulation associated with guinea pigs. The heads of real guinea pigs were filmed later, to match with the movements of the actors; these were then combined in post-production with the bodies.

The advert was run on terrestrial television and all major cable and satellite channels from November 2005 through 2006. After one month of print and internet marketing and two weeks of television advertising there was a 4% increase in brand awareness and an achievement of 111% of the sales target set. Whether the benchmark was set high or low, clearly Egg achieved the targets it set itself with its awareness campaign.

However, the point of this case study is not whether the promotional tactics were successful, but that believing promotional awareness is a separate activity that does not relate to customer service and other forms of customer communications throughout the company. The four Ps methodology does not adequately address the 'word of mouth' power of existing customers. If your brand values are claimed to be caring and open and reiterated in your promotional activity, then that must transfer to every area of the company, especially your interface with customers.

18 months after the advertising campaign, Egg wrote to 161,000 of its cardholders (presumably some of whom had been persuaded to take up the card following the guinea pig adverts), informing them that their cards would stop working in 35 days due to their "higher than acceptable risk profile". There was a substantial amount of press coverage about Egg's actions, which many claimed exceeded the coverage of the previous advertising.

Meanwhile the anecdotes, blogs and furious letters from those Egg customers with significant assets, who had never exceeded their credit limit and paid off their balance before the due date, continued to mount. An example, was Emma Baczkur[22], a nurse from Peterborough who set up a Facebook group about Egg, after she received a letter saying that it was cancelling her credit card account. She said: "I received a letter from Egg saying that it was cancelling my card and I wasn't happy about it as I had always made payments on time. I think it was cancelled because Egg wasn't making any profit from me, which made me really mad."

Her Facebook group, charmingly titled "Egg and Citigroup can shove their credit cards up their *****", attracted dozens

---

[22] *The Times*, April 2008

of members within days and played host to a lively debate about Egg's actions. She further commented: "I set up the group on the day I got the letter and invited my Facebook friends to join. Then other people I didn't know joined. The group makes it clear that everyone is fed up with the situation – we are not going to keep quiet when they say we are bad customers when we're not."

It is claimed that the decision to withdraw cards even in a credit crunch, was a grave marketing blunder that left a brand image built over ten years on friendly service, honesty and accessibility, in tatters. The 'word of mouth' power of the customers who feel they had been wronged, was substantial and has seriously dented the Egg brand and its potential future customer base for years to come. An Egg spokesman was quoted in the press as saying "even if they are up to date with their payments, they are people we no longer wish to lend to, regardless of their status." Nice touch.

PLACE

The final killer punch

The choice explosion, over supply, chronic price pressure and media fragmentation are all elements that show the flaws of the old four Ps methodology. As a consequence of these incredible things bubbling up at the same time, it's fairly obvious that the choice of suppliers and 'where' you can buy stuff, would multiply beyond belief too. *Place* as:

> *"all the company activities that make the product or service available to target customers"*

obviously remains a key marketing decision. What wasn't so obvious, was the weird distribution combinations it spawned. So intense is the competition for the contents of my purse, I can now get a DVD player from Sainsbury's, electricity from British Gas, fried chicken from Burger King, a settee from M&S, freshly baked croissants from BP and home insurance from Tesco.

But the final killer punch for the four Ps, is not the complex mix of supply options, it's one that doesn't just give it a black eye, but destroys the philosophy stone dead. It's the incredible and accidental invention that is the internet and the corresponding convergence of digital technology. I can get all these things and much more from visiting the shops or business in question, but most significantly I can probably get everything I need in life without ever leaving the house, by using the phone in my pocket, or from the chair that faces my home computer.

I haven't gone to a travel agent since 1998 but I've been abroad dozens of times. I've bid on e-bay for a variety of stuff and my books come from Amazon – not the rainforest but the website. One of my friends hasn't gone to a supermarket for so much as a bag of carrots for three years; Waitrose kindly deliver her weekly shopping with a one hour timeslot for arrival on her doorstep. I don't buy CDs anymore. I go to i-tunes, snatch a listen, and just download the tracks I like and play them on my i-pod. (If you think that makes me a technical wizard and somewhat hip, believe me you're wrong because Apple sold a million of them every fortnight during 2005[23], *a million*! And even The Queen and George Bush have one).

These are the actions of a middle-aged person who left school before computers became an everyday reality. What about people that weren't born in the 1960's? Everyone under thirty has been intimately entwined with new technology almost since the day they were born, let alone today's 18-year-olds who were born in the 1990s. Half of them have their own website pages on Facebook showing how drunk they got at Wetherspoons last Friday. They post their own spliced videos onto YouTube and communicate not by speaking, but texting in a weird language that defies spellcheck. They do all their research via the internet and some have even created a parallel 3D persona on Second Life, or publish what they had for breakfast on Twitter. Sad, but true.

I have had to learn this technology mid-way through my life. But they're the real maestros who control new technology, rather than be led by it as if by a guide dog, as I am. They have ADSL lines pumped into their houses like an umbilical cord providing a lifeline to the rest of the wired world. Teenagers today have been brought up on text messaging, MSN, The Matrix, MTV and PlayStation, not hopscotch, Mary Poppins, Thunderbirds and Ludo. If you're not convinced that this technological age is with us to stay, consider this[24]:

- 32 million adults regularly use the internet and whilst online buying is in its relative infancy, many begin their purchase with research and comparison, even if they subsequently complete a buying transaction by more traditional means.

- In the last year 29% of adults have listened to radio via digital television and 15% via radio stations online.

---

[23] iPod digital music player sales – 6.2 million March to June 2005.
[24] Combined statistics from Forrester Research, Ofcom and Ipsos MORI

40   Naked Marketing

- Between 1999 and 2003 time spent online increased eight-fold. Between the same period, time spent on mobile phone calls tripled and text messages increased fifteen-fold.

- 6 million Brits visit an internet social networking site (such as FaceBook or MySpace) at least once a month.

- 85% of UK adults use a mobile phone and 63% use text messaging.

If you have the budget ignore these solid statistics, pull the wool over the eyes of your senior executives, government paymaster or the Board, (who after all, were probably born in the 1960s or before) and go for blanket television advertising on ITV. But 20% of TV ads are skipped by viewers[25], (they don't tell you that when you buy the space). That must be far higher amongst younger people and children if they've got their hands on the remote. They're also highly sophisticated in their reading of all types of media, and cynical with it.

EMAP concluded as far back as 1994[26], in their teenage survey that; "the youth of the nineties are an extremely advertising literate bunch. Having been bombarded by billions of advertising messages since babyhood, they have increasingly high standards. Hugely appreciative and enthusiastic if an advertisement hits the right note, teenagers can be downright cynical if it doesn't..." Those same viewers today are the 25 to 34 year old bracket, who are even more media savvy, and have lost trust not just in advertising claims, but in TV voting and competitions after a series of scandals. These were worth 13% of the £1.1bn market in premium-rate phone services in 2007, with two-thirds of this age range having taken part[27].

GMTV and Channel 4's Richard & Judy, which accepted competition entries that had no chance of winning over a period of years, were given fines of £2 million and £1.5 million respectively.

---

[25] Interactive Advertising Bureau, (2004)
[26] "Youth Facts 4", Millward Brown International for EMAP (1994)
[27] Fathom Partners for PhonepayPlus, 2007

The BBC was fined £50,000 over a rigged Blue Peter competition (is nothing sacred?) and faced sanctions over phone-ins to some of its biggest charity appeals including Comic Relief and Children in Need.

If you have the budget it's easy to send out blanket adverts across all the networks and get your message across through pure repetition. But beware, your audience, especially the young, are cynical of your advertising claims. Without such budgets it's harder work, but either way you just cannot avoid making informed decisions based around robust customer research. You've got to find out what your customer segments already watch, hear or interact with, and make sure you capitalise on it and can be seen there. If your senior managers want you to advertise in the *Daily Telegraph* and do some PR to get you on Radio 4 because that's what *they* like, even though your target market read *Hello!* magazine and listen to Galaxy Radio, they're wasting their money. In all honesty they're just massaging their own egos, and if you're a marketer it's your job to give them the evidence (research) that shows where you need to be.

DON'T TRY THIS AT HOME

Marketing disasters – place

Music industry meltdown

In the last couple of years rock bands have been promoting themselves, and using the internet to share their music without the aid of big record company executives. Radiohead released their seventh album, *In Rainbows*, announcing it could be preordered and downloaded perfectly legally for as little as 1p at www.radio-head.com. A few weeks earlier the Charlatans announced they would be giving away their new album as a free download, and the rock band, The Crimea, did the same. In July 2007, Prince gave away 2.5 million copies of his new album on the cover of a Sunday newspaper. The old distribution model, where you listen to a music track on the radio, and then go and buy the CD at a music store in the high street has irretrievably broken down.

The advent of i-tunes and other music sharing sites, means that most people don't buy a whole album anymore anyway, they just snatch a listen to the tracks they like and only download those. The impact on the bottom line of the record labels has been catastrophic. When Virgin released the Spice Girls' debut album in 1996 the company made around £5 in profit on each copy sold. That margin has since shrivelled to around £2, and that is only for the big hitters. Most bands don't make any money at all for their record companies through CD sales.

It may sound odd but giving away free downloads and CDs makes good business sense. They are being used as promotional tools to sell concert tickets and fan paraphernalia, such as t-shirts, which still make money. The reprioritisation in recent years of live music over the recorded variety has been dramatic. Attendance at big music arenas in the UK rose by 11% in 2006, with around 450 music festivals taking place in 2007. TicketMaster reported that 20,000 tickets for the Spice Girls' first reunion concert at London's O2 arena sold out in 38 seconds, (why?). Glastonbury sold 135,000 weekend passes for the 2007 year event within two hours, taking more than £21million in the process. In the same year Madonna charged £160 for the best tickets at her Wembley Arena concert and the Rolling Stones £150 at Twickenham.

Given the more lucrative appeal of music tours, Madonna has left Warner Music, her record label since 1983, to sign a $120 million deal not with another record company, but with a concert promoter. Live Nation will have the exclusive rights to promote her worldwide tours, which will give them access to her ticket sales, allow them to sell her merchandise online and license the Madonna name.

With downloads, merchandising and live concerts sales now taking precedence in the music industry, CD sales are currently in freefall all over the world. UK sales have dropped 10%, with a 15% slide in the US, 25% in France and 35% in Canada. HMV has announced that its profits halved in the first six months of 2007. The Chief Executive, Simon Fox commented: "Our markets are changing profoundly. Entertainment is being generated and consumed in entirely different ways putting pressure on traditional retail space and traffic." He added that efforts were under way to "reduce our dependence" on the sale of physical music such as CDs[28].

When the private equity firm Terra Firma bought EMI recently it paid roughly a third of what the company nearly fetched during a mooted sale ten years ago. Over the same period its workforce has shrunk from more than 10,000 worldwide to 4,000. In addition Richard Branson has decided to dump Virgin Megastores, which have reportedly lost more than £50 million in 2007. The music industry is in crisis, and yet the big players had ample opportunity, and plenty of warning, to change their business models. Many of them now openly admit they were too slow to experiment with alternative distribution methods and technical developments to open up new revenue streams. Now they are fighting for survival.

---

[28] BBC News website, 27 June 2007

THE FOUR PS FUTURE

The black eyed Ps

If the Ps have been fatally wounded and are now somewhat black eyed and redundant, there needs to be a new set of guidelines. Logic surely dictates that starting with the *product* first, then the *price*, followed by *promotion* and *place* doesn't give anyone a competitive edge, and most organisations need it, because the fight for business keeps getting tougher and tougher. If you're going to just survive, let alone prosper, there's only one starting point in this weird wired world, and that's with the customer. It applies to services and products alike, and I'd argue the public and charitable sector too if you want to win hearts and minds. Marketing and sales must be truly customer-centric, although really great companies holistically use this premise to organise and deliver the whole of their operations.

A new process model for marketing must approach every step from the customers' viewpoint, not from organisational convenience. Marketing personnel must make sure that they are the voice of the customer inside the organisation – all day, every day, especially at the point management decisions are made. For example, the finance department could decide that it's more efficient internally to use a certain payment method for goods or services sold to your business customers. But is that helpful to your customer base? Is that the way they want to pay? Are you eventually going to lose your business because you've made a decision for organisational convenience? It's absolutely the marketing department's internal responsibility, to find out and express customer preferences at the point of management decision-making even when it means doing battle with the Finance Director.

Although I was an academic in a university for only a short while nearly a decade ago, I have pretty much read everything there is on marketing theory, but I've always come away with the feeling that theories are just that – theories. They have grains of truth running through them, but they're written up in sterile environments. The incredibly intelligent and insightful writers of marketing books, try to make sense of, and articulate, methods from good practice and corresponding developments in the macro-environment. But the theories are not developed from being knee deep in the middle of the white heat panic of everyday business life. I never felt that they were practical in that step-by-step sort of way. As in "here's what you do in your first month when you arrive at a new job." Or "try this if you don't have a marketing department but want to make sure you're in with a chance against the competition."

The model I have worked with in the last ten years therefore, hasn't been produced in that type of academic sense. It's from experience of the private and charity sector, big public companies, product and service delivery, trial and error, and just plain gut instinct.

The process in which I most believe, resembles partly the theories offered by Chekitan S. Dev and Don E. Schultz[29]. But as with most American business stuff, theirs loses a little in translation and British culture and conditions do vary from across the Atlantic, more than is generally acknowledged. There are parts of it that are over intellectualised and I think there are a few bits missing. But you wouldn't really know about that unless you were up to your elbows in marketing dilemmas with the CEO wanting more sales, and the company accountant trying to cut costs by homing in on the marketing budget. I call my working version Isaiah Logic, and if you read it dispassionately and look at the logic, it really is a route map for success and irrefutably shows that the Four Ps is redundant.

---

[29] Dr Chekitan S. Dev, Professor of Marketing at Cornell University, Don E. Schulz, Professor of Integrated Marketing Communications at Northwestern University. See *Marketing Management*, (Jan/Feb 2005)

PART 2

WHAT TO DO INSTEAD

ISAIAH LOGIC INTRODUCTION

Isaiah Logic á la Naked Chef

This customer-centric marketing process is stripped down to the bare essentials and stands for

- **I**nsight
- **S**olution (development)
- **A**wareness
- **I**nformation (gathering)
- **A**ssessment
- **H**andover

It's logical marketing for practical people with the theory firmly planted at the beginning of the 21st century, when things are tough. The concept can be used whether you're experienced in marketing or not, because it's just good sense. You could say that the Isaiah Logic process is simplistic, but it's better than following the four Ps, winging it, or paralysing marketing output by being overly complex. It's not anally prescriptive, but it does rely on an evidence base without becoming statistically constipated. Most of all it's practical and I've turned around some pretty desperate corporate situations by using it.

I like to think of it in the style of the Naked Chef recipe books by Jamie Oliver – hence the term naked marketing. OK he's really irritating, but when he first started, he tried to strip cooking down to its basics, make it look simple, get rid of the mystique and the snobbery, so that everyone felt they understood it and could give it a go. The recipes are really only a guide, and they're there to inspire you, and give you confidence, so that in the end you start personalising and experimenting around the edges. You gradually become a better cook, and you graduate to harder and more complicated dishes. That's what the Isaiah Logic process aims to do, so that even if you aren't involved in marketing operations you can be engaged and have an informed opinion and debate. You gradually learn and move on to a more sophisticated level step-by-step, in which case you need to move on to those academic marketing books.

The main logic is that **the customer takes centre stage** in any organisation, be it a commodity consumer products manufacturer, a producer of big ticket capital items, a business-to-business service, hospitality provider, charity organisation or even the public sector trying to engage the public along with a complex array of stakeholders. The satisfaction of those 'customers' is key, as is their positive promotion of the product, service or public campaign message they have received via *word of mouth* recommendation. So it's about providing a product, service or experience that your customers want to indulge in, buy (in its widest sense), or use, (not what you want to offer). Making information available to them when and where they want it, and giving them an outstanding customer or response service.

But most of all, Isaiah Logic is common sense, and as someone once said, *"the trouble with common sense, is that it's not all that common."*

In essence, the process asks the following critical questions based around your customers' needs and wants, and this book attempts to give you alternative solutions, depending on your circumstances and budget . . .

- **Insight** – do you know your customers?
- **Solution development** – can you solve their problems?
- **Awareness** – have they heard of you?
- **Information gathering** – where can they find out more?
- **Assessment** – how do you compare to the competition?
- **Handover** – what are you like to deal with?

Get these six elements right, and you will have a marketing plan for sustained success, no matter what business you're in.

But there's one catch if sustained long term success is what you're after – you have to be completely naked. That is, you have to be authentic, honest, fair and transparent to make it work.

THE MODEL

The Isaiah Logic Model

The Isaiah Logic Model has six stages, the first three are sequential and are generally accepted as bona fide marketing 'activities'. The final three are very different: Information gathering, assessment and handover may not always apply and even if they do, may even happen within seconds of each other, but that is no reason to ignore them. Traditional marketing books often stop at awareness, and miss out the most important one of all – handover.

It depends on your type of business and your organisational marketing needs, whether you go through each of these last three in sequence and how much time elapses between each one. If you are a retail operation it is feasible that information gathering, assessment and handover happen in a matter of minutes, and they become 'fused' in the process. If however you are selling a service, capital goods, a message or a product that involves more than just pocket money, it is likely that your customer (the public or a business client) will go through each stage, sometimes with weeks or months elapsing before they make a purchase decision.

No matter what your situation, it is still a good idea to understand these three elements, because even if they are 'fused' in the mind of your customer, you can still control their experience of each, and better influence their decision making.

The really important point about this model, is that marketing is not just to create awareness and get your customers interested. This is absolutely *not* the point, though many would have you believe otherwise. It is just one step in the process. Marketing exists purely to secure a customer – whether they buy your product, service or message. So that sales, donations or the number of people who join a campaign, volunteer or change their behaviour (such as stopping smoking), is the aim and key measure of success. You may conduct a public relations exercise, place some advertising, take your clients out for a bit of corporate hospitality and so on, but all those things are done to get you to the end point, not for their own sake.

It doesn't just end there. You may well secure a new customer, but can you keep them? If they buy something and the service is terrible or the product deficient, would you really expect them to come back again? Most people wouldn't, and in general they won't tell you that what they received is rubbish even if you ask, they'll just quietly make a note not to deal with you again, and of course they'll tell all their friends. But if you make customer service a real priority you will get repeat business, which is much more efficient than spending loads of marketing money on finding new business. You will not only make a customer, but reach the marketing nirvana of making an advocate. Someone who will, through word of mouth (the best advertising of all), spread the message about your superior product or service, or in terms of charity and social marketing become an ambassador for your cause.

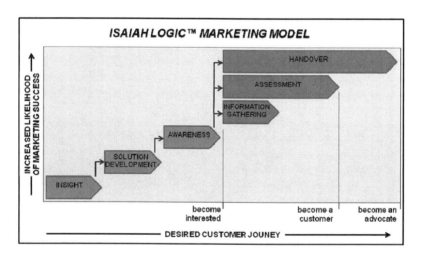

If you make changes to the way you do business and your approach to marketing, by following the six part process, you will make advocates out of your customers, which can only increase your chances of success.

PART 3

DO YOU KNOW YOUR CUSTOMERS?

INSIGHT EXPLAINED

A job for nosey parkers

If you're sold on the concept that the customer (or audience) is the start of the equation, then you have got to understand everything about them. *Everything.* You have to start here, or how else can you make any type of business decision, let alone marketing decision? You need to be a nosy parker about your customers and the market that surrounds them, or pay someone else to be. Although this technique is used reasonably often in public-facing private sector organisations, it can also be applied to profile professional buyers of services or for business-to-business customers. If you work in the public or third sector and you are trying to campaign to change behaviour, it is absolutely essential. Sometimes this sort of approach is classified under wider theories on customer relationship management or market research, but *insight* is a good description of what you're trying to achieve, and it's easier to understand.

Even if you don't follow the advice below you should at least analyse what is working. If you run a promotion and it works, do you know why and how are you going to replicate the success? As the former Chief Marketing Officer of The Coca-Cola Company[30] put it:

"...very few people anywhere in business are very diligent about analyzing success. We take success for granted. When we measure results and find we are ahead of plan, we just decide that the assumptions we made were very smart and that we no longer need to worry about finding any additional justification for what we did . . . Don't be blinded by your assumptions. Just because you run a promotion and it works doesn't mean that it worked for the reasons that you thought it would."

---

[30] Zyman, Sergio (2000), *The End Of Marketing As We Know It*

Aside from debriefing promotions or advertising campaigns, how do you decide what to run in the first place? Are you risking your marketing investment because you're just guessing?

Insight is the starting point and one of the most valuable marketing tools. In some ways it is nothing to do with your message, product or service, it's about your potential customers' attitudes, behaviours, lifestyle, life stage, preferences, spending power and views. Initially, you should divorce it from your intended message, commercial output and service or product offering and profile them as people. You must not assume that because someone is a particular age profile that you automatically know what everyone else at the same life stage thinks. Or worse, don't for one minute believe that because, 25 years ago you were a 20 year old, you have a handle on what it's like to be that age now. You really don't.

The 'big shed' out of town operators such as the supermarkets and DIY suppliers, and the financial services industry are generally the most sophisticated users of insight. If a big shed retailer wants to build a megastore, it takes a huge amount of capital investment so they have to put a robust business case to prove that a particular locality will give a good return. They use tools such as Mosaic[31], (which is a fusion of 6,000 sources of data including the latest census, mortgage lending figures, household debt and credit figures and so on), to help pinpoint where the new store will have the best chance of success.

When cross-referenced geographically and demographically it can tell them how many potential customers are within walking distance, how much disposable income they have, where they go on holiday, which newspaper they read, what car they drive, whether they own a DVD player, how many houses in the catchment area have a garage, how many people of what age live in each household, etc., etc., ad infinitum.

Mosaic profiles all 24 million UK households down to 243 segments. Far too sophisticated for the marketing requirements of most companies, but for a big retailer it can help clarify not only if

---

[31] Marketed by Experian and developed by Professor Richard Webber, a leading authority on consumer segmentation. Also similar is CACI's Acorn research tool

the capital investment of a new store is viable, but help decide on product ranges and pricing strategies. After all if car ownership is low in the area, the store needs to be on a bus route and car polish won't be a best seller. And if no-one has a garden in the vicinity you wouldn't provide barbecue-ready food in the deli section during the summer, or give shelf space to charcoal and firelighters.

Some companies delve into complex psychological profiles of their customers or draw parallels with Maslow's *Hierarchy of Needs* model, but unless you're in a multi-million pound hyper-competitive marketplace that's probably not necessary. Mosaic and similar research tools can be expensive or too detailed, but there are many research organisations that can carry out bespoke surveys at a reasonable cost, delivering profiles of a handful of customer segments. Even research conducted yourself could provide useful insights.

Doing it yourself might sound odd, but it's better than nothing, and will at least give you a feel for your customer base. If you don't have enough money to employ an agency, you can still do your own research by investing a little time and thought. I'm always shocked when someone puts their life savings into a new shop. It opens locally and closes a year later. This is old fashioned four Ps thinking, putting the offering or product first and hoping someone will buy what you sell – pushing outwards towards the customer. If they had just gone out into the street with a clip board and some basic questions; got to understand who lives in the area, what they spend their money on and when, what lifestyles and opinions they have, they would have minimised their risk of failure, because they would have known what products they preferred, when to open, pricing strategies and so on. Successful businesses that have thrived from the start without spending a few hours on these basics are just plain lucky. I just wouldn't want to bet my redundancy money, savings or credit facility on lady luck.

No matter whether you spend a fortune on detailed insight research or your information is pretty basic, the most important reason for starting here, is to construct customer segments or profiles. You just can't treat all your customers as one homogenous mass. Taken to the extreme, a teenage boy will want a different product with different qualities and a different design than a 70 year old great aunt. They look at the world differently, use different language, access different types of media and want different things from life entirely. It's very unlikely that they're going to want exactly the same product or service, and even if they do, they don't want it presented and promoted to them in the same way.

A regional airport in the UK, gives a good example of the use of profiling. They wanted to work out what services and retail offerings it should provide after check-in but before getting on the plane. This airport has really smart management, and instead of just enticing loads of retail outlets into that space and leaving them to flog their goods, they wanted to profile airport customers and use the research to give travellers the outlets and services they wanted. Customer first, not product.

They didn't just look at their customer base and lazily split them into age groups, assuming (say) that all people in the 18 to 24 age range are going on holiday and want to booze at the airport. They paid for research that gave an insight into passenger attitudes. What they found was the total customer base divided into a handful of attitudinal segments. There were the (generally) single sex groups of varying age, who were on holiday the minute they arrived at the airport. They were outside their normal family set up, had saved up and they couldn't wait to spend spend spend. They wanted the wait between boarding to be a part of their holiday experience, and above all they were excited and intended to have a good laugh.

There were business travellers who used the airport an awful lot. They ranged from the professional, well-paid, ambitious, but relatively young executives of either sex, to the more elderly statesmen-like, 'old school tie', male board members who were semi-retired. This segment wanted to be as far away as possible from the 'holiday' customers. They wanted the minimum hassle and peace and quiet. They rarely bought anything at the airport and they wanted a slight recognition of their status, because they were there so often. Another segment hated the airport experience and ideally would like to drive their car to the bottom of the plane steps and get straight on.

Naturally there were other segments too, but the point is, the research the airport carried out, wasn't designed to find out what their customers actually wanted to buy, or the services that they wished to receive. First, they wanted to profile their customers and get some kind of understanding of what it's like to be them[32]. They wanted that insight so they could design around them. Ultimately that would lead, of course, to higher spend per individual.

If you do your own research, you can construct some pretty unsophisticated segments, but even these will help increase business. If you own a café, you may notice that young mothers visit in the mornings, but it's mostly office workers at lunchtime, whilst there are a distinct group of elderly people who come in late afternoons. What do they order, what do they need and how much do they spend, have they got certain attitudes to some of your product or service offerings? Write these down, and begin to decide on menu items, the facilities you provide, speed of service and pricing policies at different times of the day. Alternatively, you could just treat them all the same, but you won't increase your income significantly, and your café will be up against some stiff competitors who have thought it through.

Because of the changing nature of the macro-environment that affects most businesses, I would argue that this type of research will only be relevant for three years, maybe four at the most. It's then best to wipe the slate clean and start researching all over again. That way you stay ahead of the competition and have the information to keep feeding organisational innovation. It's a zero-based marketing approach.

---

[32] It can be helpful when carrying out insight research, to get an illustrator to draw up how the different customer segments might look, or create a photo montage, and also to give them a name that epitomises their attitudes and behaviours. This gives a graphic illustration (literally) of the different types and shows the contrasts between their needs and wants. It's really useful to use these illustrations inside the organisation as it breathes life into the research and is a powerful tool to help staff to focus on, and understand, the reasoning behind later strategic marketing decisions.

Synopsis

Insight is the power to discern the true nature of your existing or future customers

The result of insight research is a profile of your customers including their economic, social, demographic and psychological characteristics and their behaviours, whims and preferences. It's also useful to profile their use and response to a variety of media – magazines, tv, radio, posters, text messaging, etc. Therefore by its nature the act of customer profiling will contain a variety of factors and lead to the development of groupings (or segments). One tier segments, for example simply based on age are simplistic and often irrelevant. The segments become the aggregation of a set of prospective customers that have common needs and will respond similarly to marketing messages. The use of insight research to form segments, leads to strong clues to the motives behind their actions, the best media to choose and helps predict reactions to your product/service/message and marketing activity.

HOW TO GAIN INSIGHT

Where to get the best

As discussed, there are many types of research that may help your organisation. The case study on supermarket geodemographic profiling, shows how key segments can be built up to gain invaluable insights into your existing and potential customers. This type of work crosses over into the area of solution development, because if you find out about your customers and profile them, (to better target them in the future), you are obviously going to want to find out their predisposition towards new products, developments, services or add-ons, too.

If you can afford to use a good marketing research agency (note – marketing research, not market research), that is to say an agency that doesn't just give you stats, but gives you research to inform your future marketing, then they can profile your customers for you in as much detail as you can afford. They will also make very strong recommendations about the marketing channels that will work best for each customer segment. This is 'actionable' information, not pages of numbers that leave you wondering what to do next. Good marketing research will help you make key decisions to inform a comprehensive marketing strategy. It will allow you to better target and keep your existing customers and increase their level of sales, but it also means that by understanding the current customer profile you can seek out similar new customers.

For example, if you know that owner-managed technology businesses that have reached a turnover of around £10-15m and have grown rapidly in the last five years, are most likely to buy your product X. And that the buying decision-makers in those companies tend to go to a specific exhibition each year, or read a particular magazine, it becomes very obvious how to use your marketing budget to get to them. The segmentation work also shows you the product benefits that most impress them, and the level of pricing they are comfortable with. Not only do you know who you are targeting and where, you know what to say in your marketing literature and in your one-on-one sales pitch. Your insight research of existing customers, gives really good clues to sell to new ones, and where you can find them. Strange that so many companies don't work out the basic profile of their current customers, and use it to find similar ones.

This type of work can cost huge amounts, depending on the level of detail you require and how complex your business. However a workable segmentation could be accomplished for as little as £60k, maybe even £30k, but it would take an agency at least ten to twelve weeks to deliver the final research report. If that sounds expensive, consider whether you are spending marketing budget on a campaign that isn't backed up by evidence. How do you know it's going to work? If the campaign costs £50k and you don't know who you're aiming it at, why or where they are, you're wasting your money. So why not cut out one of your marketing projects and replace it with the research instead?

On a budget

With a small budget you can employ a market research agency to conduct some interviews for you, and create the type of customer segments as explained above. Good agencies will carry this out thoroughly, so that the results are statistically viable, however it can be done without such cast iron evidence. This method will give you hints as to the likely segments, not ideal but much better than not doing it at all. However, it must be stressed that the agency does not have enough quantifiable data to prove the results or tell you how large the segments are. They will not be able to 'stand by them', but they will be able to give you really useful draft segments.

A likely methodology is to conduct twelve or so, in-depth telephone interviews with a selection of your customers. If they can create outline segments from this, they can then recruit further customers and conduct three or four focus groups to attempt to verify and add depth to their findings. This should give you a reasonable segmentation at a cost of around £15 – £20k, and good information on their price sensitivity, their needs, wants and attitude to your products and services. In turn, this gives vital clues to inform a full marketing strategy, with defined tactics for increasing sales for each of the different clusters that make up your customer base.

If times are hard, cash flow is tight and you can't afford to go down this route, you could do it yourself, as shown below. This is never advocated in marketing books but surely it is better than just guessing what your customers want, and wasting your marketing budget by not understanding why your marketing activities either do, or don't, work:

1. Establish a sample of customers which represent the different decision-makers found in your market. Make sure they are a representative sample in every way possible (without being impractical), such as geographical split, distribution method preferred, size of company, product or service preference, average size of purchases/orders, etc.

2. When you have a representative list (needs to be about 120 in size, if you have that many customers), decide what questions you would really like to ask them. How do they make their buying decisions? What do they like about your service and what do they hate? Don't forget you need to know personal things about the buying decision maker – what media they use, magazines they read, how many staff they have, how senior they are and so on. Collate these into a clear and succinct list of questions.

3. Appoint someone (internally or externally) who is good on the phone and get them to ring your list of sample customers, and book an appointment with them to go through the questionnaire. Ensure that you do not take up more than 10 to 15 minutes of their time. From the target list of 120, you will need a total response of at least 20 to 30 customers or more, depending on how complicated your business is.

4. A small team will then need to go through each completed questionnaire, to collate the findings and see if they fall into distinct categories because they give the same types of answers. Construct profiles of them and define the service elements or products that they are most interested in, how price sensitive they are, how they prefer to receive marketing information and so on.

5. Finally, in constructing segments of existing customers, you also have a defined profile of new customers, by size of turnover or industry sector, or a whole host of other characteristics. By doing this, you can buy company lists or scan other sources of information to construct an inventory of targets for new business.

Where this tactic generally falls down however, is not in conducting the research, but lacking the will or effort to do something with the information gained. This work must be used to make fundamental decisions, and changes if necessary, to the approach, targeting, marketing and selling of your service or products. Using, not gaining, this vital information will give you the edge over competitors and lead to sustained profits and new business. If this is what your customers are telling you, your long term survival is at stake if you ignore it.

Market research agencies

The Market Research Society (MRS) has a website that includes a "Research Buyers Guide" at www.rbg.org.uk.. This is a directory of market research providers and support services. You can search for a supplier in your area or use the Bulletin Board to post a notice with details of your market research needs. All companies listed are Full Members of MRS, ensuring compliance with their strict Code of Conduct.

Recommended further reading

- Wilson, A. (2006), *Marketing Research: An Integrated Approach*
- Bradley, N. (2006), *Marketing Research: Tools and Techniques*

You can find some useful information on market research agencies on the Business Link website, under the *Sales and Marketing* heading, visit www.businesslink.gov.uk.. They have a market research guide which you can download free, and lots of other related information although it tends to be for the smaller business.

INSIGHT TOOLS

Whilst you should be conducting some form of insight yourself to really get a feel for your customers, or for whether your product or service solves their problems, there are also some reports that are available off the shelf. They are usually very expensive to buy, but could prove much cheaper than commissioning your own, especially if you just want a generic market background. Make sure that the report is reasonably up-to-date. With the business environment changing so quickly, anything that was conducted more than three or four years ago is unlikely to remain relevant. Below are some examples.

Geodemographic information

You can buy the Mosaic or Acorn systems which give detailed information on profiles of members of the public by geographical location, down to postcode level. You can even buy a mapping system to pinpoint them. Its uses are described in more detail in the Supermarket case study and on their respective websites[33]. You can look up a limited number of postcode profiles for free to get an idea of the sort of information available.

Market reports

Detailed analysis of a number of markets are available to buy off the shelf. The two most well-known companies that supply market reports are Data Monitor and Mintel. They both offer intense analysis of sub-sectors of a market, for example they provide reports on the wine market in Spain, UK couriers or global software

---

[33] www.caci.oc.uk/acorn and www.business-strategies.co.uk for Mosaic

sales. Data Monitor also has detailed reports of individual companies, trends analysis or specific markets in individual countries. Reports can cost from a few hundred to a few thousand pounds, and can be downloaded or sent by post as a hard copy.[34]

Target Group Index and National Readership Survey

The Target Group Index[35] (TGI) survey typically covers 18 broad product/service areas, providing data on 4,000 brands in over 500 product fields. The sectors covered include alcoholic drinks, food, snacks, household products, toiletries, cosmetics, pharmaceutical products, DIY and gardening products, electronics, financial services, motoring, holidays, travel, sport and leisure. It is based on answers to questionnaires that can take up to four hours to complete. There are 500,000 people who take part in 38 countries in local languages, and reports are released quarterly. Because they are so detailed they can be analysed in terms of product categories, demographics, attitudes, beliefs and preferred media channels.

There are many similar tools such as the National Readership Survey[36] (NRS). This involves personal interviews (some 35,000 plus per year) with a representative selection of members of the public. Interviewers call at selected addresses and interview one or two adults in each household which on average takes just under 30 minutes. These surveys are designed to provide estimates of the number and nature of the people who read Britain's newspapers and consumer magazines. They provide an estimate of the number of readers of a publication and their type in terms of sex, age, regionality and many other demographic and lifestyle characteristics. This is used by publishers of newspapers and magazines, advertisers and advertising agencies principally for the purpose of planning, buying and selling advertising space.

You can subscribe to the data or have specialised reports cross referenced and prepared for your business category. These can give

---

[34] Visit www.datamonitor.com or www.mintel.com
[35] www.tgisurveys.com
[36] www.nrs.co.uk

profiles for consumer products (and other categories) in the case of TGI, or to make decisions on where to place advertising, and is certainly better than having no information at your fingertips. It is not as helpful for complex service businesses or the public sector. However, if you do use it for media selection or consumer marketing, the data is inevitably skewed, because it relies on a certain type of person who is prepared to either fill out questionnaires for hours on end, or have an interviewer in their house. Because of their propensity to get involved in this process, these people cannot be representative of the population as a whole.

Socio-economic classification

This has to be the most outdated marketing tool of all, nearly as bad as the four Ps methodology. I have no idea who invented it, but it probably belongs more in the 1950s than the beginning of the 21st Century. Unfortunately, it is still used to classify readership of newspapers and magazines, and the results or targeting of other marketing media, because there simply isn't anything currently available to take its place. I have included it here because you will come across it, even when we live in a complex social structure that no longer conforms to past generalisations of class divisions. For example, if you wanted to place an advert in the Financial Times, the publishers would give you a breakdown of the readership by class to see if that fits in with your potential client base. In this case it is most likely to be predominantly ABs (see below).

The ABC social grade classification is determined by the occupation of the Chief Income Earner (CIE) in each household. Additional criteria such the size of the organisation and the number of people for which the CIE is responsible, are used to refine the process. The generally accepted description of the six grades is as follows:

Social Grade	Social Status	CIE's Occupation
A	Upper Middle Class	Higher managerial, administrative or professional
B	Middle Class	Intermediate managerial, administrative or professional
C1	Lower Middle Class	Supervisory or clerical and junior managerial, administrative or professional
C2	Skilled Working Class	Skilled manual workers
D	Working Class	Semi and unskilled manual workers
E	Those at the lowest levels of subsistence	Casual or lowest grade workers, pensioners and others who depend on the state for their income

If you come across these, you now know what they're supposed to mean.

Stakeholder analysis

A stakeholder is any person who can have a positive or negative impact on your business. Stakeholder analysis, typically looks at identifying these people, with the aim of keeping them informed of your activities, to try to foster cooperation and understanding. In some instances, this could be with the express aim of successfully delivering a single project. For example, if your organisation builds houses and you were applying for planning permission, it would be important to identify key individuals from a range of backgrounds to engage in the process, including environmental groups, planners, residents, members of the local council and so on.

There are many methods of stakeholder mapping, but the one

used most often proposes a classification of stakeholders based on power and influence[37], it includes the legitimacy of each stakeholder's relationship with the organisation, and the urgency of the stakeholder's claim on the organisation. The map is then used to draw up a strategy to prioritise and organise regular communications to keep them engaged.

The simple Power-Interest grid (below[38]) is one way of mapping your stakeholders into four boxes and then deciding on the communications you need to keep them engaged. For example stakeholders in Box A, may only need monthly e-newsletters and putting on your general mailing list, whereas those in Box D will additionally need personal visits, invitations to company events, etc.

A Low Power and Low Interest *Minimal effort*	B Low Power and High Interest *Keep informed*
C High Power and Low Interest *Keep satisfied*	D High Power and High Interest *Key players*

---

[37] Mitchell, Agle et al. 1997. Also see Fletcher, Guthrie et al. 2003 (mapping stakeholder expectations based on values) and Savage, Nix et al. 1991 (classifying stakeholders according to potential for threat or cooperation)
[38] Mendelow (1991)

INSIGHT EXAMPLES

THAT'S THE WAY TO DO IT

Real life insight examples

Black Holes and Uncle Albert[39]

Professor Russell Stannard wanted to write an entertaining book for young people that would help them learn about physics, especially Einstein's Theory of Relativity. He knew that if he asked young readers their criteria for a great book that they would enjoy reading, they were unlikely to be able to articulate the separate elements. He decided to find out about their needs by measuring their behaviour and finding out what they really wanted.

To do this, he spent many hours in the local library looking through children's books and counting up the date stamps to see how often they had been borrowed. He analysed the most popular books and listed all the features that he believed they had in common such as illustrations, lots of dialogue, humour, short chapters and characters the readers could identify with.

He also needed to know how much children might already know about the subject, so he could pitch the book appropriately to them. He surveyed 250 twelve year olds and worked out their awareness and depth of knowledge on topics such as gravity. He then wrote his book *Black Holes and Uncle Albert*. He sent his manuscript to 18 publishers before it was finally accepted. Since then it has become a popular bestseller.

---

[39] Taken from the Virgin Business Guide book – Wolff, J. (2001) Do Something Different

THAT'S THE WAY TO DO IT

Real life insight examples

Supermarket geodemographic classification

You would think that if you bought a pint of milk it would cost exactly the same in Sainsbury's as it does in Tesco, and to get the best value from one of the biggest expenditures we make across the year, we would shop around between supermarkets. We don't. The British have a tribal attachment to specific supermarket chains, and some would argue it even identifies your class. Tesco, the implication goes, is for commoner people than those who shop in Sainsbury's. Waitrose is for those more likely to have second homes in Padstow than the first two. Asda for people who aspire to have a second home anywhere but probably never will. Lidl for people who have never heard of Padstow. Marks and Spencer for those who have never heard of Lidl.

Demographically profiling customers is hugely important to the £75 billion supermarket industry, which is a cut-throat business with a handful of hugely powerful competitors, who have managed to get us to buy all our food in their shops or on the internet thereby wiping out the once prevalent corner shop. There are constant ferocious battles waged on price cutting, additional services and location, and those that understand their customers best, come out on top. None of the supermarket chains would dream of opening a new store or initiating a price promotion without using swathes of geodemographic analyses.

Verdict Research for instance, has found that Waitrose has the highest proportion of high class shoppers from the professional social classes (47%), followed by Sainsbury's (34%), Marks & Spencer (22%), Tesco (21%) and Safeway (17%). At the bottom of the market, 72% of Netto's shoppers are blue-collar workers, with Kwik Save (66%), Lidl (54%) and Somerfield (50%) close behind.

However, the old fashioned definitions of class are no longer flexible enough to be of use to supermarkets, when deciding where to locate their stores or whether to move the beer next to the nappies after 6pm (as some do), when mums have run out and dads are sent to get them. To help in the decision making there are two key products in the market, which essentially offer the same type of analysis. One is called Mosaic and the other Acorn, and most supermarkets use them to help make key decisions. The systems use the 2001 Census figures and data on hundreds of statistical sources such as county court judgements, salary levels, credit ratings, qualifications, mortgage data, car ownership, age and background.

This fusing of data allows a supermarket to analyse its catchment area, know how far people will travel by car or whether they will use public transport, whether their homes have a garden, what food they will eat at what times of the day and year, how much they are prepared to spend on categories of products, whether they will like background music and what it should be, what age their kids are, what times they need to be open because of working patterns, and so on.

Acorn categorises all 1.9 million UK postcodes, showing residents as one of 17 groups with descriptive names such as "affluent greys" or "burdened singles". They further break these down into 56 types within those groups. For example the "flourishing families" group has four types; larger families in prosperous suburbs, well-off working families with mortgages, well-off managers in detached houses and large families and houses in rural areas. By tapping in a post code you will instantly access the type of person who lives there, their likely income, family situation, spending habits, age and even whether they make donations to charities – and which ones.

Both Acorn and Mosaic also have a mapping facility which will then allow the supermarket to plot the residents within their catchment area, and work out their geodemographic profile and subsequently their shopping needs. The system is also used extensively by the financial services sector, local government, NHS and others to help make informed decisions on where direct marketing and advertising campaigns will be most effective, where branches should be opened or closed, or where retail outlets, leisure facilities or public services should be located.

THAT'S THE WAY TO DO IT

Real life insight examples

Regional UK airport

Some years ago a regional airport in the UK, decided to refurbish and update its airside retail, leisure and business provision. The brief was to re-think the retail offering after passport control and before boarding, and to re-design waiting areas. However instead of letting out space to the highest bidder, the airport commissioned qualitative research from agency Marketing Works, to better understand its customers, provide better designed waiting areas and leverage higher spend.

Marketing Works came up with six distinct segments, shaped not by age, gender or wealth, but by behaviour. The four most prominent are shown below:

Fun, Fun, Fun

For this segment the holiday begins at the airport and they enjoy virtually every aspect of the airport experience. They have every intention to spend, spend, spend.

A to B

These are a functional group. They see flying and time at the airport as an inevitable inconvenience which eats into their holiday time. If they could they would drive their car up to the plane steps and board.

So Sensible

They view the airport as a source of irritation and expense; a 'conspiracy' to get them to spend money. They would bring their own food and drink if possible and have no intention of buying anything.

The Professional

Frequent business travellers who spend their time at the airport working. They need space and facilities and even though many don't travel business class, they would like to have their status recognised.

This information had obvious benefits for the re-positioning of its whole airside offering. Armed with this insight they could, not only offer a retail experience that suited the profile of its customers, but look at the facilities their customers most wanted, and could confidently design seating areas, business sections and other public areas too.

DON'T TRY THIS AT HOME

Marketing disasters – insight

Marks and Spencer

I am a great admirer of market research, indeed I've used it extensively, but statistical techniques alone are of limited value to marketers. Well actually that's not quite true. Stats give factual evidence and great quantitative analysis. A sort of *state of the nation* report, statistically verified. It's a barometer and a crystallising of social issues and their current state. It's a sophisticated answer to a "what" question or a "who" or "where" question. Sometimes the research gives us clues to "why", but what we need to know more than anything else is "how". If that's what it's like out there, then *how* do I develop a product or service solution, *how* do I change public behaviour, and *how* do I construct marketing messages that convert to a sale?

Your sales director can no doubt give you detailed figures on last month's sales, but the real question is why are they above/below/the same as the previous month, and how are we going to do better? I know from MORI, for example, that litter and dog fouling is more important to local people than education or health. But clues on how I can get people to stop littering and stop allowing their dogs to foul are far more pertinent. In essence it's easier being a market researcher than someone responsible for marketing and sales, because they have no responsibility for having to do something with the stats they unearth.

When I was little, my grandmother knew everyone down her street. A professional nosy parker in fact. A natural market researcher. In later life she took great pride in going to Marks and Spencer for her clothes. To her it was very upmarket – a measure of her, rather restricted, social mobility. And yet, her devotion to M&S faltered towards the end of the 90s. It seemed to have lost touch, not only with her generation but it wasn't attracting younger shoppers either. The clothes, famous for their quality, just weren't so good anymore. Their higher prices were no longer justified and they stubbornly refused to take credit cards, only their store cards. My grandmother's loyalty was severely tested and she stopped shopping there quite so often.

M&S would have commissioned lots of research during that period – sales figures, trends analysis, statistics on almost everything. The stock market gurus would have predicted future share prices, whether to buy or sell and so on. And yet suddenly M&S fell into an unpredicted slump, which took the company and nearly all retail analysts and business journalists, by surprise. The company's share price fell by more than two thirds, and its profits dropped from more than a billion pounds in 1997 and 1998 to £145 million in the year ended 2001.

So why didn't they know it was coming? It probably didn't help that most of the Board were white middle class males. When did they last go shopping for women's clothes, or for anything for that matter? I think it's not that they didn't do their research, I think it's that they died of paralysis by statistical analysis – constantly looking at the what, when and where answers, and not exploring the how, with the people who knew best. They had become completely disconnected from their customers, commissioning market research and not insight. If they had walked down the street and asked people like gran what they thought, they would have spotted the signs and could have made corrective actions to their product range and their service, and saved their reputation and shareholder value.

DON'T TRY THIS AT HOME

Marketing disasters – insight

Tropicana

Most commentators and marketing professionals will argue that even when a fast moving consumer brand, most notably the ones sold in supermarkets, are well recognised by consumers, you have to keep making small tweaks to keep it relevant. Carefully and slowly updating every couple of years, so that consumers never really notice. The trick is for their favourite package on the shelf to remain strangely familiar and yet completely up to date. However, sometimes a company will decide they want revolution and not evolution.

PepsiCo decided to go for a bit of revolution with the Tropicana Pure Premium brand at the close of 2008.

Typically, a well executed visual change to a high profile product, signals increased marketing expenditures and leads in general to improved sales performance, maybe not in the long term, but certainly in the short term, mainly because of the novelty value. It gets people to look at the brand again, and if they haven't bought it for a while, brings some kind of news and excitement which leads to them giving it another try. As to loyal repeat buyers, they too recognise the increased effort and continue their normal buying patterns.

Tropicana sought to create such excitement around the *Pure Premium* rebrand, announcing on 8 January 2009 an "historic integrated-marketing and advertising campaign … designed to reinforce the brand and product attributes, rejuvenate the category and help consumers rediscover the health benefits they get from drinking America's iconic orange-juice brand."[40] These were tough times, and clearly PepsiCo thought that they needed a boost. The entire refrigerated orange juice category posted flat unit sales and a 5% decline in dollar sales during that period. After its package redesign however, their unit sales dropped 20%, while dollar sales decreased 19%, or roughly $33 million between Jan. 1 and Feb. 22[41]. In addition, several of Tropicana's competitors appear to have benefited posting double-digit unit sale (including Minute Maid a Coca-Cola company) increases during the period. Private label products also saw an increase during the period.

On the 23 February, the company announced it would bow to consumer demand and scrap the new packaging. It had been on the market less than two months.

---

[40] Advertising Age, 2 April 2009
[41] Information Resources Inc.

Given a loss of around $33million in just seven weeks and the huge cost of commissioning a new design, let alone adjusting manufacture to the new package, why did the marketing research commissioned to see if consumers liked the new design, get it so wrong? Or did they decide to save money in this department and not bother?

PART 4

CAN YOU SOLVE THEIR PROBLEMS?

SOLUTION DEVELOPMENT EXPLAINED

More Eureka moments please

Once there's a much greater understanding of the customer as a human being, the second stage is to work out if they have difficulties and problems with the types of products, services or experiences that you, or others, offer. This highlights the threats and opportunities for product and service provision. There is a real crossover here with insight activity. In the regional airport case study example, it became easier to spot the types of customer and analyse their movements or interview them to help solve their issues or problems.

In a more general way, here is a small sample of some old potential customer dilemmas:

- "Switching the grill on every morning, waiting until it gets hot, putting two pieces of bread under it, watching for when they get toasted, turning them over and browning the other sides – I love toast in the morning but it's driving me mad."

- "I hate washing up after a meal."

- "I need to be available on the phone when I'm on the train and in the car."

- "I need to catch a really early train in the morning and I know I'll be in a hurry. You already have my credit card details why do I have to waste time checking out at the reception desk?"

- "I keep forgetting to turn the kettle off when it's boiled."

As the great Harvard marketing professor, Theodore Levitt, put it, "people don't want quarter-inch drill (bits). They want quarter inch holes." It is therefore essential not to segment your market around the product or service, and not to develop new products or services around the nuances of drills. It's the feature and function of the hole that you're after. Make sure you are not asking the wrong questions because you'll only solve the wrong problem.

So it's not about delivering innovative products, or developing new services, it's about finding solutions to customer dilemmas. But the catch is, customers don't give quotes like the ones above, it's rare for them to be able to identify and then articulate those problems, let alone offer up a design or service solution. To discover customer problems and work out innovative solutions, organisations must go beyond traditional market research techniques. Competitive advantage and stunning profits can be made, if you can constantly anticipate the future requirements of customers, often when they haven't yet worked it out themselves.

To do this, you cannot just whizz out a questionnaire or participate in an omnibus[42] and think it will lead to innovation nirvana. Potential customers generally cannot tangibly express their needs, because they rest at a sub-conscious level. Direct questions don't help at all, they just make people think along the lines that you've established for them. How many times have you got a stats report back from a research agency, and the answers seemed strangely familiar? It's because old fashioned quantitative market research generally reflects common knowledge, or even what the public *thinks* you want to hear.

The honest truth about being stopped in the street by someone with a clipboard, is that people don't tell the honest truth. On lifestyle questionnaires the public systematically exaggerate or under-report their behaviour. Would you really admit exactly how many units of alcohol you drink each week, or that you drop litter? Of course not. If you were a fifteen year old lad, would you agree that you had already had sex and that you smoke cigarettes? Of course you would.

The inclination to be economical with the truth and hide your

---

[42] A national survey, typically carried out weekly by a large market research agency (e.g. MORI), with face-to-face interviews with the public on a very large scale. Companies can construct a few questions of their own, and pay to add it to the larger survey.

real thoughts extends to questions about your voting intentions in elections. Every single poll claimed that John Major would lose the 1992 election and that Neil Kinnock would be the next Prime Minister. It seems that lots of people didn't want to admit they were going to vote Tory, even when asked. In January 2008 during the democratic nomination race, the media anticipated an Obama Barrack triumph in New Hampshire following his comfortable win in the Iowa caucuses just five days before. It was reinforced by polling data that showed, without exception, that he was firmly in the lead. When the votes were counted Hillary Clinton had won. A substantial proportion of white voters felt uncomfortable saying that they wouldn't be voting for a black guy.

Sadly many organisations have yet to realise that the straight 'pollster' approach is practically obsolete for businesses. It's OK for opinion polls (if you understand their fallibility) or finding out the 'state of the nation', but not to inform new product development or service solutions and marketing decisions – it has too many flaws.

We have to delve far deeper to develop unique innovative ideas, because the point is, they're not ordinary. Every definition of innovation from Drucker[43] onwards focuses on the concept of newness:

"(Innovation is) an idea, practice, or object that's perceived as new by an individual or other unit of adoption."[44]

And as succinctly stated by Marquis, as early as 1969:

"recognition of demand is a more frequent factor in successful innovation than recognition of technical potential."

He knew that by its very nature "new" is original, so you cannot ask 1,000 people to agree what a revolutionary new product should be, or what new sort of service they want. You won't come up with no-frill airlines, the Post-it Note or the widget in a beer can, doing it that way. I mean think about it, would a focus group of eight people

---

[43] Drucker, P. F. (1985), Innovation and Entrepreneurship
[44] Rogers, E. M., (1995)

brought together in Crewe for two hours, be able to invent text messaging for you? Of course not. But the arguments of Marquis go further; we shouldn't be doing straight market research or customer profiling, we must put mechanisms and responsibilities in place to identify and predict demand, otherwise we are destined to be a market follower.

Breakthroughs come from ridding ourselves of linear thought processes and resisting the temptation to painstakingly track our way using step-by-step thinking. Even then, unless you can predict demand, and your solutions fill a need, gap or problem in your customers' lives, they're not going to buy or use it. For front line customer service delivery (such as reception services) this is particularly pertinent, but it also applies to product or more general service provision: You might want to deliver, and have the expertise, for self service terminal check-ins for hotel guests, but if your customers have to wait longer and they feel it has no perceived value and they're just not interested, forget it.

To develop a marketing strategy, demand needs to be predicted and the 'hidden problem' identified, and then defined in minute detail. Only then can a solution 'fall out' of the future context and definition. There are many ways of doing this but three of my own personal favourites are empathic research, extreme user research, the development of behavioural customer segmentation with an additional constant of trends reporting:

Empathic research: get out there and see how customers truly interact with your service or product, or your competitors services. It's about seeing the world from a user perspective, understanding the problems they face and their tacit requirements. Often this simply involves clandestine observation or doing 'mystery shops'[45]. You can pay research organisations to do this, or use anthropological experts if you have a very technical product, but I think using your own staff in some way can make a huge impact as

---

[45] Mystery shoppers pose as normal customers performing specific tasks, such as purchasing a product, asking questions, registering complaints or behaving in a certain way. They then provide detailed reports or feedback about their experiences.

they start to see what it's like from the user viewpoint, an essential element for improving customer service.

Extreme user research: this is research with customers who have more extreme service or product requirements than the average user. For example, someone with hearing problems, language or mobility difficulties. I like to do this even if you don't have really extreme users, as it makes the NPD or marketing team think more widely about the implications of their new product or service delivery choices. For example, can a left-handed person use your new potato peeler, or how does a person in a wheelchair get to their restaurant table? It also helps them to be more innovative when revisiting existing products or services.

Behavioural customer segmentation: this usually involves focus groups (it sounds a bit New Labour but read on), with a statistically viable mix of your defined customer segments, which follow a gentle semi-structured interview script. Usually this is carried out by highly experienced practitioners, who are trained to use the insights you have already gained. They recruit people who epitomise the segments you have drawn up (see the previous pages) and probe their attitudes in more depth to gain behavioural knowledge based around the product or service you offer. It partly uses observational methodology and can use complementary or different products, services or experiences to identify hidden needs and make broad recommendations for problems that need solutions. For two examples see the case studies in the Insight section on supermarket geodemographics and the regional airport. However, you can conduct this research yourself to really define your existing customer base, their reaction to your marketing activities, their needs and wants, etc.

Trends reporting: is an important additional constant to the above and is largely a desk top exercise. Whilst the other three define customer problems and tease out new product or service responses, trends reporting looks much further ahead into the future, trying to articulate market trends and predict future demand. Using a mix of statistical data and observing competitor moves, trends reports should identify macro-environmental issues that will affect future customer provision. These reports draw hypotheses on trends and extrapolate scenarios to give clues to future strategy setting and hence the context for shaping new product and service development.

A simplistic example is climate change. As an issue it is progressively influencing public attitudes and behaviours. The government has increased company car tax and the road tax disc is more expensive for cars with higher CO^2 emissions. If you were a car maker how is that going to affect future production and sales? Recycling and re-use is becoming more prevalent, should you adopt an environmental policy to show your customers your green credentials? Will that positively affect their perception of your company and thereby gain more sales enquiries? The key is to spend time anticipating the things that will affect your customers' attitudes to your product or service in the future, not just copy everyone else when it becomes mainstream, so it looks like you're jumping on the bandwagon.

The general public and business customers are deluged with new products or services every week – they're overwhelmed. Marketing, R&D and design departments are obsessed with the next new thing, churning out pilots or prototypes based on customer questionnaires, volumes of statistics, subjective gut feelings and who knows what. But new product failure rates are increasing. Perhaps you should forget the next big brainstorming idea in respect of marketing and development, and systematically focus on solving customers' problems and observing market trends. Like IBM you can then start to offer 'solution bundles', which tie into strategic corporate objectives.

This approach will give you more Eureka moments, and transform your organisation and your thinking from being mere suppliers of products, services or experiences to proactive solution providers. It gets you much closer to your customers and enhances your knowledge of them. Only then can you diagnose their challenges and work with them to craft appropriate solutions.

Whilst the first element is essentially evidence-based, the solution can be, and should be, as creative as possible. You should encourage thinking along non-linear lines and reward brave solution decisions, as long as they really do solve your customer 'problem'.

Synopsis

Solution development is the act of revising existing, or creating new, products, services or experiences that solve customer problems.

Solution development falls into two distinct halves. First, is the scientific analytical ability to recognise and carefully define gaps, problems and difficulties for potential and existing business customers, using strongly evidenced based observations, market trends and part of the insight research. The second is to be outrageously creative and brave to develop innovative service and product solutions to problems. The two approaches must go hand-in-hand if innovation is to be commercially successful.

HOW TO DEVELOP SOLUTIONS

Where to get the best

The majority of new products or service models that are launched with a fanfare, will fail and everybody accepts that (sort of). But the risk of failure can be reduced by establishing a sound new product/service development process. Although there are variations, the basic process includes ideas generated then screened, evaluated in more detail, developed, tested and finally launched. Ideas can come from anywhere and everywhere, but it is an essential part of this book's thesis to begin with the customer, and not dream up new products or services in glorious isolation. An ingenious new product can easily be the best, but that doesn't mean people will want to buy it. Just think of the British motorcycle industry to remind yourself to look outwards and not inwards.

The process of new development is not a linear sequence of events with a start and finish. Results from tests, customer feedback and general discussions make it a series of loops, where over time you strive to make the new product, campaign message or service better and better. There are many organisations that will do the whole new product or service development process for you, including trends analysis, depending on your budget. This can be really useful if you feel you need a completely new approach to what you are doing, someone with fresh eyes that is independent and unhindered by company history and politics. Some specialise in industry sectors, others are more generalist.

On a budget

If you run a huge factory that makes products, where tooling is an enormous expense and a key part of the process, it is likely that new product development is fairly well established internally. You just need to ensure your approach is based around identifying and solving customer problems, and not production-led. However, if you provide a service or make products on a smaller scale, or without the need for tooling and expensive machinery, you may need to conduct solution development activities in a more modest way by yourself.

It is surprising how many people sell their service and product, but never ever go out and see how a customer uses it. Even if you are the owner, you should get out there and see how customers truly interact with your service or product, or your competitors' services. Do you really know what it's like to deal with your staff or use your product? This will cost you nothing other than your time, but will give you essential information to improving all aspects of your business. If you don't want to do that, convince a friend, or task a member of staff, to conduct a 'mystery shop'[46]. This may sound very 'private sector' but it applies equally to the public sector. How do patients interact with NHS services, or a resident with the local council? It's just as relevant.

As mentioned in the *Insight* section, you could also conduct extreme user research to test the limits of your service or product, and it is a good idea to conduct trends reporting every six months or so. To compile a trends report appoint a member of staff, or pay a consultant, to conduct a desk top study looking at future developments that may have an impact on your business. Get them to articulate market trends and predict future demand by identifying macro-environmental issues that are outside your control but could affect future customer provision. The traditional process includes examining possible legal, ethical, technological, political, social, economic or environmental developments. You need to be one step ahead to ensure a new law won't devastate your business, or that technological advances will make your offering redundant within a couple of years.

---

[46] Mystery shoppers pose as normal customers performing specific tasks, such as purchasing a product, asking questions, registering complaints or behaving in a certain way. They then provide either anecdotal or detailed written reports or feedback about their experiences.

Product and service development companies

This is a difficult one, as there are so many different types of organisations offering products and services in a variety of industry sectors. However, there are two websites which may be useful. Design Partners can be found at www.newdesignpartners.com. They showcase design consultancies in the field of product design, and usually have around 80 listed across the UK. Each one has a profile, with contact information and examples of work.

Depending on your requirements you may prefer a consultancy that specialises in ergonomics, and the general way in which customers physically use your products. The Ergonomics Society has a website at www.ergonomics.org.uk and has a directory of its registered consultancies. Each one listed, gives details of their location and specialist areas.

Recommended further reading

- Karol, R., Nelson, B. (2007), *New Product Development for Dummies*
- Ulwick, A. (2005), *What Customers Want: Using Outcome-Driven Innovation to Create Breakthrough Products and Services*

You can find a trends analysis tool on the Business Balls website at http://www.businessballs.com/pestanalysisfreetemplate.htm

The Design Council also offers some good articles on a variety of design disciplines including product design, service design, retail design and so on. Go to their website at www.designcouncil.org.uk, click on the "about design", and then on the "design disciplines" link.

SOLUTION DEVELOPMENT TOOLS

To get sustained sales you need to create services and products that solve people's problems. But the way you create the 'look and feel' around the service or product or even the name of your organisation is an important element. Customers will assess the product or service by its initial look and feel, it gives them huge clues as to whether your company will be good to deal with, whether they are professional, have integrity and give good value for money. Developing a brand to fit your offering is the way to express your corporate personality.

But, there is a lot of confusion between the meaning and use of the terms brand, branding, corporate identity and logo. Naturally there is no definitive meaning, but the interpretations below are the more generally accepted notions. As a client or marketing professional it is important that you agree the meaning of these words, so that you are not at cross-purposes. The understanding of the implications of each is essential in making decisions about product and service development and the overall marketing strategy.

Logo development

Generally this is the word used to describe the visual combination of the company name and sometimes an accompanying graphic or symbol, which is used on all marketing and other materials. It should be simple, distinctive and easy to recognise. Some logos have symbols which are so strong and identifiable that the company name isn't even included. Visualise the Red Cross, Playboy, Mercedes, Shell and Nike logos. Some use only type to give them their distinctive appearance, such as Kellogg's, Coca-Cola and Harrods. It is helpful to think of your logo as the mark of an old fashioned branding iron. It shows everyone what you own, so that they don't confuse your goods or services with anyone else. Whilst the original meaning of a brand was just that – a hot iron seared into the side of cattle to identify ownership – branding has gone on to mean so much more (see below).

Some logos are not distinctive at all, and are in fact incredibly bland. Sainsbury's, The Financial Times and the BBC have their own corporate colours but no graphic device and indistinct typefaces. This explains the difference between logo and brand most clearly, because whilst you may have difficulty recalling the exact logos of these organisations, you know their values, culture and precisely what they stand for. The logo is just a mark, but it's the stuff around it that creates a whole identity.

Some companies mistakenly think that they need to re-design their logo when a new boss arrives, a change programme is initiated, or they just want to appear more modern. This is often not necessary. If your logo is clean and simple and is recognised by your clients or potential clients, (i.e. the opposite of the 2012 Olympic logo), leave it alone. What you need to work on is your branding.

Brands and branding

In the old days branding used to be called corporate image, which to be honest is a better description and more easily understood but obviously doesn't sound as sexy. Everything in the Isaiah Logic process is aimed at gaining a fantastic reputation through word of mouth recommendation. The modern concept of brand is an attempt to explain the experiential and psychological aspect of dealing with an organisation or its products or services. The first is often described as the brand experience, this means every customer contact with the company, its people and outputs. This aspect has been thoroughly discussed in the Awareness and Handover sections, and particularly emphasises how the quality of that delivery must be authentic and real. All too often in marketing campaigns, a great brand experience tries to be artificially manufactured by advertising agencies with unrealistic expectations raised, because whilst the product or service is successfully promoted, the other services or delivery around it bears no resemblance to the actual customer experience. The marketing campaign therefore only delivers a short term sales increase. What those agencies most want, is to work for an organisation that really is superb at customer service and experience, so that they can genuinely highlight it.

The psychological aspect of brand image, is a symbolic construct created within the minds of consumers and consists of all the information and expectations associated with a product or service. The visual representation of the company, its logo, sales literature, retail space, etc., is an embodiment of this overall feeling towards the company. The job of the directors at the top of an organisation, is to align the expectations behind the brand experience, and make sure it happens in reality. The brand image therefore goes on to develop a personality in the consciousness of consumers. Whilst, as mentioned above, the Financial Times has a non-descript logo, the pink pages of its newspaper, the size of its pages, financial information on its website, the adverts, photography it uses, the style of journalism, the use of type and so on, create a very strong corporate identity or brand. It's serious, upmarket and influential. It's the whole package that gives it that feel, and if I rang up their reception desk, which I've never done, I wouldn't expect a Jade Goodey (rest her soul) soundalike to answer the phone.

It's not just the logo that creates that original impression, it is too insignificant on its own. It's not enough to have a lovely visual image and expect that to deliver satisfied customers. It's all the other visual clues and experiences that create, what is described as brand recognition, which organisations are trying to achieve. If the experiences are good and the collective visual mechanisms are distinctive, the combination results in brand value. If that value or reputation, can be positively built over time the whole thing goes full circle. That little logo, which once was just a mark of your branding iron, becomes the total embodiment of all the experiences and psychological aspects of doing business with you. It becomes the symbol of everything you stand for. It's very valuable and sometimes described as brand equity, although in Isaiah Logic we have used the term *reputation*. In tangible terms, brand equity, goodwill or reputation, is the amount someone would pay for your company over and above the black and white of your financial situation.

If brand value has been built up successfully and the organisation feels it has reached a plateau regarding sales, or it wants to capitalise on its brand equity, they will often attempt brand extension. They feel the name is so strong it can be pushed into other areas, in which it hasn't traditionally done business. This is dangerous because if the move is unsuccessful it could diminish the core reputation. The most obvious example is Virgin. Having created a strong identity and reputation in the music business, Richard Branson extended the brand into air travel, and has since also expanded into rail travel, finance, mobile phones, internet and so on. There are many others who have used their existing strong brand name as a vehicle for new or modified products. For example, many fashion houses have extended their brands into fragrances, shoes and accessories, home textiles, luggage and sunglasses. Mars extended its brand to ice cream, Caterpillar to shoes and watches and Michelin to a restaurant guide.

Further reading

- de Chernatony, L., McDonald, M. (2003), *Creating Powerful Brands*
- Olins, W. (2004), *Wally Olins on Brand*
- Ries, A., Ries, L. (2000), The *22 Immutable Laws of Branding*

And if you want to read something that criticises the whole concept of branding and its influence on modern day society, there is of course:

- Klein, N. (2001), *No Logo*

Naming a company, product or service

If you're considering a new name for a company, service or product it could be one of the most important marketing decisions you will ever make. The choice of the name, just like the choice of your branding and styling, is not a subjective decision, nor should it be a political one. You, and your managers, shareholders or board must resist the interference of others, and choose the name for the right reasons, unfettered by anyone's own preferences, but focused on your mission and vision, and your target audience(s). The guiding principle therefore is *will our customers like it?* They are buying into your image, your company and your brand, so it's not really a question of whether *you* or the board/shareholders/stakeholders like it.

The importance of a strong and distinctive brand name should never be underestimated. A good choice can ensure your brand is memorable and differentiated. It can help with positioning and the communication of key messages. The internet is the single biggest reason for the need for internationally acceptable brand names. Increasingly confident consumers are more willing to research and purchase goods, services, and even their education, through the internet. It therefore makes good business sense for brand names to have an immediate impact, be memorable and stick in the mind quickly. In addition there are four principles that need to be 'cross-referenced' against the final choice:

- Impact
- Accessibility
- Clarity
- Global relevance

It should also be noted that if you choose a name that will be highly controversial, most especially politically unacceptable, it could have an adverse effect on publicity and staff morale. On the other hand the most successful names over the long-term are often those that initially are a little controversial or different (Google, Swatch, Ikea). Whilst it's probably wise not to welcome controversy for the sake of it, an organisation and its brand names need to stand out amongst competitors. You need to show some creativity and boldness in your choice.

Trademark and domain name acceptability

A new brand name should be registered in the trademark register of each country in which it will be used. If you feel this is not necessary it can be done solely for the UK. You can go to the Companies House website[47] to check against registered company names, to ensure there isn't a clash, but the first stop for information is The Patent Office[48]. Their website gives details of intellectual property protection. You can do a preliminary search, or you can get a company to give you an initial trademark report on the name you have chosen for as little as £50. A trademark is a sign or text capable of being represented graphically and which distinguishes goods or services. A trademark may consist of words, designs, logos or combinations of letters and/or numbers, but there are some restrictions on certain words or phrases.

Copyright is used to protect the visual identity of the design and text of your new logo. It is not necessary to register copyright, however strictly speaking it resides with the agency or person who designs the final logo, so when you place a contract for a new design, make sure there is an agreement that on payment, the copyright passes unreservedly to you.

Don't forget that you need to ensure you can get the domain name you want, too. It's no good starting with a great name like orange, only to find that every derivation of that name from .co.uk, to .com to .biz has been taken. You don't really want a domain name that ends up being www.orange_limited.com.[49]

What type of name?

Names come from a variety of sources. Many European languages are derived from either Greek or Latin, and the trend towards global markets, make these names easier to transfer across continents, examples abound including Hovis from the Latin 'hominus vis',

---

[47] www.companieshouse.gov.uk
[48] www.patent.gov.uk
[49] There are hundreds of websites where you can check domain name availability for free, and buy domain names online. Try www.lcn.com.

(strength of man) to Nike (Greek for 'victory'). Nike replaced the original name of Blue Ribbon Sports – it's easy to work out which is more memorable.

Acronyms and 'coined' names incorporating elements from one or more words are often useful tools for avoiding translation difficulties, as they are less likely to have meanings in other languages. Well-known brand names using this formula to create a new word include;

- IKEA – founder Ingvar Kampard, his farm Elmtaryd and his village Agunnaryd.
- 7-UP – refers to the seven flavours of the drink
- Persil – the product's two main ingredients, percarbonate and silicate
- ADIDAS – taken directly from founder Adi Dassler's name
- Nylon – an abbreviation of New York and London

This is a particularly effective strategy for minimising trademark difficulties. However, the inevitable human instinct to shorten any new name must be taken into account e.g. British Telecommunications (BT), British Broadcasting Corporation (BBC) or National Westminster Bank (NatWest), before making the final decision. You don't want to name your company or campaign something like Clean Up National TV (which Mary Whitehouse originally did in 1963), only to find the initials or shortened version is embarrassing or downright rude.

Whatever the naming approach, one word brands are most effective. Lengthy, multiple word names lead to truncation as mentioned above. Subsequently when people abbreviate a name, control is lost over the brand and identity.

Other naming tactics include using brand names that describe (e.g. PowerBook, Burger King, British Airways, Carphone Warehouse, Toys R Us) or words taken straight from the dictionary with no direct correlation to the service or product itself (e.g. Yahoo, Starbucks, Orange).

You can employ an agency to come up with a brand name, the most famous being Interbrand, based in London. This will of course cost tens, if not thousands, of pounds, but you may consider that a good investment depending on the size of your organisation, the strength of the competition and the nature of your business.

Additional considerations

New names should not be too constrictive and should allow for possible future strategic developments. Commerce and industry are changing at an increasingly rapid rate. It is impossible to predict macro-environmental changes with absolute confidence over the coming decades, especially those that will take effect long after you have launched a new product or service. Don't forget your ambitions too, if you grow quickly it may be too parochial to call yourselves Wrexham Engineering, you might move your main site to another town or establish other centres, not just in the UK but maybe internationally. This may be unthinkable now, but in ten years?

If you plan to sell overseas you will need to get your brand name checked by a translator. You don't want to fall into the same mistake as countless others such as Vauxhall (their Nova car name was fine in England, but in Spanish "no va" means won't go), or Toyota, (the Toyota MR2 is pronounced "Toyota Merde" in France). Others include:

- Pocari Sweat – Isotonic sports drink (Japan)
- Bimbo – bread (Spain)
- Kräpp – toilet paper (Sweden)
- Alu-Fanny – aluminium foil (Norway)
- Pantry-boy – Nissan car (Japan)
- Bonka – coffee (Spain)
- Bums – biscuits (Sweden)

A rose by any other name

Selecting a name is an emotionally charged decision. Naming decisions are fraught with politics, turf issues and individual preferences. You must stick to a strategic internal decision and not entertain the lowest common denominator solution. Along the way there is always someone who will try to derail the process. You need to determine at the outset who the decision makers will be, and then work diligently to keep the decision-making process on track.

The new name will have a degree of controversy, whichever you choose. Everyone will have an opinion, and there will be those in favour and those against. It is a classic no-win situation. Over time it will become better known. Customers, staff, stakeholders and the local community, will find it more comfortable as time passes and accept it as part of the background noise.

A rose by any other name, might smell as sweet, but probably not if it's called *Pocari Sweat*.

Recommended further reading

- Taylor, N. (2007), *The Name of the Beast*
- Rivkin, S., Sutherland, F., Trout, J. (2004), *The Making of a Name: The Inside Story of the Brands We Buy.*
- WOW! Branding (2007), *Logo Savvy: Top Brand Design Firms Share Their Naming and Identity Strategies.*

ANALYSIS TOOLS

A new product or service should be developed with the user in mind, looking at how to solve their problems and come up with innovations that persuade them to become a customer. But it's no use coming up with something that someone else has already developed, or that your fiercest competitor can copy in an instant. As always, models, theories and principles are over-simplified representations of a complex, many layered reality. In most business professions there are academic writings that try to create order and process out of the chaos of working life, and marketing is no different. These can be really helpful when learning new ways of working or trying to maximise your chances of new product or service development success.

Below are some analysis concepts (though it's by no means an exhaustive list), that you may need when you are trying to make development decisions. I try to give a succinct, jargon-free interpretation which always runs the risk of over-simplification, however you can source the originals for a thorough technical explanation. They could be a useful way of seeing if your new idea will survive amongst the competition.

The Four Service Characteristics

Most marketing books centre around product marketing to consumers, as examples are easy to come by and they can be easily recognised because people will have heard of them. Developing service solutions and then marketing them, is often so much harder as the route to market can be complicated and often what needs to be sold cannot be seen by the potential customer before they buy it; take computer networks, window cleaning or holidays as an example. There are also services that are sold not to consumers but to other businesses, hence the term business-to-business (or B2B) marketing.

Service marketing texts often espouse the awful Seven Ps theory, with the additional three Ps being people, physical evidence and process. Please don't go down that route. As explained thoroughly in this book, you need to use the Isaiah Logic process in any type of marketing, but most especially for services and business-to-business because so much rests on handover (customer service).

Based on the books that were published in the 1980s[50] which realised that service marketing was different from product marketing, there are some worthwhile observations about the characteristics of services and how they need to be made tangible. In a nutshell they define four characteristics:

Intangibility

It is difficult for the buyer to evaluate the service offerings as they cannot see the final outcome or define its quality. The marketing needs to make the service as tangible as possible, showing photographs of the outcomes of the service or supplying case studies or testimonials of previous successes. Premises, staff appearance, buildings, literature and so on is important, as the buyer will take clues from their immediate experience or surroundings as to whether the service will be efficient, effective and of a good quality.

Inseparability

When you buy a product, you rarely meet the producer and mostly consume or use the product some time after you have bought it. Production and consumption are separated. Generally services cannot be separated from the service provider. Hence, if I buy legal advice, I go to receive a legal consultation there and then from a lawyer. Its consumption is inseparable from its delivery and the deliverer. Service providers therefore, must concentrate much more

---

[50] Especially, Cowell, D. (1984) The Marketing of Services and Lovelock, H. (1984), Services Marketing

on training, skills and personal delivery and developing systems and processes for increasing customer throughput.

Perishability

With products if they are unsold you can store them and sell them at a later date. However with services unused capacity cannot be saved for future use. For example, unsold seats on an aeroplane cannot be transferred and sold on the next flight, or slow periods at a restaurant cannot be saved up for a Saturday night when more people want tables than are available. The key for service providers is to try and manage demand by efficiently servicing busy periods and incentivising customers to visit during downtimes. Tactics include differential pricing (e.g. happy hour) and developing complementary services.

Variability or heterogeneity

Because service marketing is so reliant on the quality of staff and how they deal with your customers, it is extremely difficult to maintain consistency and quality. There is a strong possibility that the same enquiry could be answered slightly differently by different people (or even by the same person at different times). It is important to minimise the differences in performance through training, standard-setting and quality assurance, and develop strong customer care programmes and systems.

Product Life Cycle and Adopter Theory

Once you have developed a new service or product and bring it to market, you will want a big advertising fanfare, but what will happen after that? There is a firmly established theory that once a product or service reaches the market for the first time, it enters a 'life cycle' where eventually it will fade and be withdrawn from the market[51]. This period of time, can vary dramatically from a matter of

---

[51] There are also theories surrounding 'technology lifecycles', this has a different curve and applies to an entire technology or a generation of a technology, not a single product or service.

months to decades. The theory was developed in the 1960s by Raymond Vernon, but obviously not every market offering will fit nicely into each of the four headings.

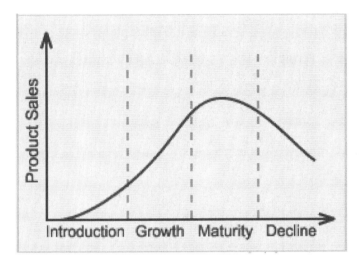

This was first used to explain international trade, but has latterly been bastardised by marketing professionals. Primarily it has been used to analyse sales figures to decide where the product or service sits on the product life cycle curve. By doing this you can decide when best to initiate a marketing blitz or refine or modify it, to keep the product or service as near to the top of its sales peak for as long as possible. If you have a portfolio of fmcg products, like Cadbury's for example, you cannot pay for mass marketing campaigns for each of your products all the time, it's not financially viable. By examining the sales curve and pinpointing when sales have dropped to a certain level, you can initiate the advertising blitz. This is done in the belief that if you let sales dip too low from their peak it becomes too difficult to revive them. In practice then, the curve should rise and fall in small waves during the maturity phase. Once it consistently hits the decline curve, it may not be worth investing in marketing activity, instead transferring the expenditure to another product or service offering that's in one of the other three life cycle phases.

The drawback is that the shape of the curve is misleading. Some products hit a market and look more like a pyramid – spectacular initial sales upon launch, followed by a small peak and a decline that is equally as dramatic. Examples would include the Xbox, or other technology products which ride on a 'fashion' storm and disappear when the next new innovation reaches the market. At the opposite end of the scale are products such as Heinz Tomato Ketchup, Kit-Kat or Marmite, which seem to have been around forever and are still going strong. The key is not to use an established theoretical model, but to define the shape of *your* market's/product's sales curve and decide on 'trigger' points when you want to initiate marketing action.

There is also said to be a relationship between the product life cycle and the 'adoption' of the product by buyer type[52]. Along the same shaped curve consumers can be grouped into five 'adopter' categories, each of which has a distinct characteristic. Upon the introduction of a new product, a small number of consumers (typically less than 3%) categorised as *innovators* will take the risk and buy, even though the product or service has yet to be proven. *Early adopters* will buy the product as it gains popularity, but has yet to reach the mainstream. As marketing campaigns increase awareness and word of mouth recommendation spreads, sales will increase to a peak during the growth stage, with the *early majority* buying. As product popularity begins to tail off slightly, the more cynical will be won over by the evidence and the *late majority* will buy. Finally when the product is in decline, there may be price offers and other incentives and that is when the *laggards* finally purchase.

Calculating market share
Calculating market share could help decide if product or service innovations are working, or whether you need to invest in more

---

[52] Roger, E.M. (1962), *Diffusion of Innovation*

solution development. But an increase in sales figures is not necessarily a reliable indicator, as it does not automatically mean a company is performing well in relation to the competition. For example if a new product is launched that is replicated by a number of players, such as MP3 players, and the whole market grows by 500% in one year, and yet your company records a leap in sales of only 200%, you are falling drastically behind the competition. However, you can only calculate market share if the size of the total market is known, usually from trade associations or market research companies.

So the calculation of market share is relative to competitors, not a straight sales figure, and is measured as a proportion of total market sales, as follows:

market share = your company sales / total market sales.

Sales may be determined on a value basis (price per unit multiplied by volume of sales) or on a unit basis.

Porter's Five Forces

Porter's Five Forces[53] is a classic diagnostic tool to analyse the competitive environment. Whilst PESTLE (see below) analyses the macro-environment, the Five Forces tool looks at the more immediate external influences that could affect your sales or drive down prices: It helps you understand both the strength of your current competitive position, and the strength of a position you could be looking to move into. Generally, it is used to identify whether new products, services or businesses have the potential to be profitable over the long term, or whether you need to enter a market quickly, make a profit and leave.

Porter believed that there were five important forces that determine competitive power in a situation. These are:

---

[53] Porter, M.E. (1980), Competitive Strategy: Techniques for Analyzing Industries and Competitors

Supplier Power

How much power do your suppliers have over you, and are they in a position to drive up prices? By analysing each key input that makes up the total product or service you offer, you can determine supplier strength and their control over you and the cost you would incur when switching from one to another.

Buyer Power

How easy is it for buyers to drive your prices down, or to walk away? This can be driven by the number of buyers, the importance of each individual buyer to your business, the cost to them of switching from your products and services to those of someone else, and so on. If you deal with only a couple of powerful buyers, they can often dictate terms, as their threat of withdrawal is very serious.

Competitive Rivalry

How good are your competitors and are there many of them? If you have capable competitors and they offer equally attractive products and services, then you'll have little power in the market. If suppliers and buyers don't get a good deal from you, they can easily go elsewhere. On the other hand, if no-one else has your offering or can deliver such quality, then you have tremendous strength in the market.

Threat of Substitution

This is affected by your customers' ability to find a different way of doing what you do, or sourcing what you provide. If substitution is easy and viable, and competitors could come up with an alternative solution, your product or service will soon be under threat.

Threat of New Entry

Competitor power is also affected by the ability of people to enter your market. If it costs little in time or money to enter your market and compete effectively, especially if there are few economies of scale in place, or if you have little protection for your key technologies, then new competitors can quickly enter your market and take a slice of market share. If you have strong and durable barriers to entry, then you can preserve a favourable position and take fair advantage of it.

PESTLE Analysis

Working out how your immediate competitors and market situation (Five Forces) might affect your business so that you can adopt strategies to survive and prosper, is obviously a good idea. Another form of analysis is to keep scanning the macro-environment to be as aware as possible, of any 'big' events that might hit your company in the future. PEST or PESTLE analysis is one method to do this, it helps you to understand the environment in which you operate (external to your company or department), so you can take advantage of the opportunities for new products and services and minimise the threats against your existing ones.

A **PESTLE analysis** is a business measurement tool, often used in conjunction with a strategic SWOT analysis (Strengths, Weaknesses, Opportunities and Threats), and is an acronym for Political, Economic, Social, Technological, Legal and Environmental factors. You'll find loads of variations such as PESTLIED, STEEPLE, STEPE and SLEEPT but they all more or less have the same content.

You need to keep an eye on the factors below, to decide if any trends or potential developments could affect your business and especially how they will affect a proposed new service or product. If these pose a threat or opportunity how would deal with them if they did arise? For example, as a café owner, how will a hot summer affect you? Or a very cold winter? You probably need to consider supply problems, changes to your menu, opening hours, etc. What about shifts in attitudes to healthy eating, or the affect on personal expenditure given the economy? Or even the need for people to access the internet while outside the office? Keeping track of developments will not only keep you innovating for your customers but keep you one step ahead of the competition.

Political

Trading and government policies, funding initiatives, inter-country relationships and attitudes, internal political issues and shareholder needs and demands.

Economic

Economic trends overseas and at home, seasonality issues, market and trade cycles, industry factors, taxation, job growth and unemployment, interest and exchange rates and inflation.

Social

Consumer attitude and opinions, media views, consumer buying patterns, ethnic and religious factors, demographics, lifestyle changes, population shifts and health.

Technological

Technological developments, research funding, information and communications, innovation, technology access and intellectual property issues.

Legal

Current and future legislation in the UK and internationally, employment law, consumer protection, competitive regulations and industry-specific regulations.

Environmental

Ecological and environmental issues, customer values, stakeholder and investor values, management style, organisational culture and staff engagement.

Boston Consulting Group's Growth Share Matrix

Companies which are large enough to be organised into business units, or who have a portfolio of product/service offerings often face the problem of prioritising resources amongst these units. Should they all receive the same level of investment, or would some benefit from increased levels of funding?

In the early 1970s the Boston Consulting Group (BCG) developed a model for managing this portfolio. The BCG Growth Share matrix displays the business units/major product service lines, on a graph showing the market growth rate v market share relative to the organisation's competitors. Resources are allocated to business units according to where they are situated on the grid as follows:

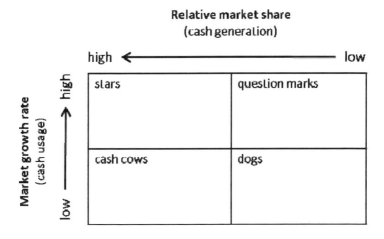

Cash cow – a business unit that has a large market share in a mature, steadily growing industry. Cash cows require little investment and generate cash that can be used to invest in rising stars and question marks (see below).

Star – a business unit that has a large market share in a fast growing industry. Stars may generate cash, but because the market is growing rapidly they require more investment to put them ahead of the competition or maintain their lead. If successful, a star should become a cash cow as the industry matures.

Question mark (sometimes called 'problem child') - a unit that has a small market share in a high growth market. They require resources to grow market share but it is still not clear whether they will become stars or turn into dogs (see below)

Dog – a unit with a small market share in a mature or declining industry. A dog may not substantially soak up cash, but it could tie up capital or resources that could be better deployed elsewhere. Unless a dog is needed for other strategic purposes, it should be liquidated if there is little prospect for gaining market share.

Overall the grid can provide a framework for allocating resources at a glance, and should include predicted directions of travel. However, this grid is based upon market share as the key business outcome, when in practice this may not lead to sustained profitability. It also assumes that market growth is beyond the control of the organisation, when it could take actions to grow the market. These criticisms are intended to be addressed by the GE/McKinsey Portfolio Matrix (see *Recommended further reading* below).

Recommended further reading
- Stern, C.W., Deimler, M.S. (2006), The Boston Consulting Group on Strategy: Classic Concepts and New Perspectives

The marketing audit
It is useful to conduct a marketing and communications audit, to give a picture of your brand manifestation in the settings that your customers will view it. Identify formal and informal communication channels and current brand usage where it interfaces with customers and stakeholders. This could include websites, social media presence, print and broadcast materials, newsletters, signage, etc. Take

photographs, print off examples and lay them all out in a room. Is this the image you want to create? Has your brand become diluted with use? Deliver an honest and open assessment of your organisation's presence as seen through the eyes of customers and stakeholders, and use it to inform future marketing strategy and how you will control how it looks in the future.

SOLUTION DEPENDENT EXAMPLES

THAT'S THE WAY TO DO IT

Real life solution development examples

moneysupermarket.com

After dropping out of Nottingham University, Simon Nixon spent a few months selling insurance and mortgage products, and realised there were no tools available for advisers to check, compare and source mortgage deals in the market. With this in mind, he launched a magazine called *Brokers Update* but within two years subscriptions had begun to plateau as brokers increasingly used computer technology to glean the information they required. He persuaded a friend, Duncan Cameron, a student in computer science to build a software program that could compare market rates. They launched it in 1994 as *Mortgage 2000* and five years later, set it up as a web-based site renaming it moneysupermarket.com.

Aside from mortgages, the website now has additional comparison areas, with over 200 'partners' who provide information on their products. Search tools are also used to obtain quotes on behalf of consumers from many other different insurers and brokers. A large proportion of the company's revenue comes from affiliate fees or commission paid by providers when users purchase their product via the website.

In June 2007 the company announced its intention to float on the London Stock Exchange. Nixon has a £375m stake and spent £162m buying out his partner Duncan Cameron. He is listed as 258th in the 2008 Sunday Times Rich List.

THAT'S THE WAY TO DO IT

Real life solution development examples

3M and Post-it notes

During the mid-1960s a 3M chemist, Spencer Silver, discovered a totally unique phenomenon – a new polymer that was only partly sticky, not "aggressively" adhesive. He was fascinated by his discovery but could not find a commercial application for it. A decade later, Arthur Fry, a 3M corporate scientist, was attending his local church, when his bookmarks kept slipping out of his hymn book. It occurred to him that it would be useful to have a "permanently temporary" bookmark that would stick to the page, but could be removed later without harming it.

Initially the, then "Press'n'Peel" pads using Silver's discovery, were tested within the company, where the staff quickly became addicted to using them. In 1977, the first formal test markets were a complete failure and the whole project was almost scrapped. But staff in the company had become firm believers in the future success of the product, and it was thought that sales were almost non-existent because people did not know what to do with them. What was needed was personal demonstrations of the product and how they could be use, and this approach was used in a new launch.

The following year, 3M changed the name to Post-it notes, and in 1980 they went into national distribution. Four years later they became the company's best-selling product, and by 1995 sales exceeded $500 million.

DON'T TRY THIS AT HOME

Marketing disasters – solution development

Sinclair C5

Most people over 40 will remember the C5 'car'. A one-seater, three wheel vehicle where you sat inside a fibre glass shell, with your legs in front of you and your backside two inches from the ground. It was developed as a result of the abolishment of tax on electric vehicles in 1980 and legislation allowing anyone over the age of 14 to drive an electrically assisted cycle without a helmet or insurance. Sir Clive Sinclair the inventor, had already achieved success with a number of new products including his executive pocket calculator, and wholeheartedly believed these two cracks in the law presented a personal travel opportunity.

He openly admitted that he did not believe in market research, but still managed to get backing for his new car/bicycle concept with predicted sales of 100,000 units a year. Launched in 1985 and priced at £399 it was to be sold through mail order.

Aside from a lack of market research Sir Clive didn't trial the marketing of the car either. When it was launched to the media on a slippery, snowy day in London on a very hilly site, journalists were not overly impressed. The Consumers Association tested the C5 and warned that on the road it was the same height as the bumpers of other cars, and this made it difficult to see and increased the chance of accidents. Further they pointed out that its low height meant that exhaust fumes, spray from rain and dazzle from headlights were in the direct line of vision of the driver. The journalists also noticed there wasn't a reverse gear, the top speed was 15 mph, the battery only lasted for 15 miles and drivers had to pedal up hills because the motor kept cutting out.

After three months production was cut back by 90% and eventually stopped altogether after six months.

DON'T TRY THIS AT HOME

Marketing disasters – solution development

New Coke

In the mid 1980s, Coca-Cola was feeling under threat from Pepsi, who were making startling gains in market share, with a 2.5% gain or around $500 million in lost sales, in just four years. They believed that the Pepsi-Cola drink was increasing its sales because consumer taste had transformed; towards a slightly sweeter flavour.

Naturally, a huge cultural and consumer icon could not be changed on a whim and risk reputational and sales damage, so Coca-Cola decided to test a new sweeter formula, which they described as "New Coke". They spent $4 million on market research just to make sure.

The change was announced to the media on the 23rd April 1985 with over 200 TV and newspaper reporters attending the glitzy launch. It included a question and answer session, and a history of Coca-Cola. The debut was accompanied by an advertising campaign that revived the Coca-Cola theme song of the early 1970s, "I'd Like to Buy the World a Coke". But they didn't explain why they made the change and did not make reference to the extensive taste testing they had carried out.

The change to the world's best selling soft drink was reputedly heard by an amazing 81% of the US population within 24 hours of the announcement. Within a week of the change, one thousand calls a day were flooding the company's information line. Most of the callers were shocked and outraged, many said that they were considering switching to Pepsi. Within six weeks, the switchboard was being jammed by 6,000 calls a day. The company also received over 40,000 letters of protest, (luckily this was before e-mail was a common communication currency). Their market share fell from a high of 15% to a low of 1.4%.

Pepsi were overjoyed that the Coca-Cola company was changing its secret formula. They declared it as a decision that recognised that Pepsi tasted better. Roger Enrico, the president and CEO of Pepsi-Cola wrote a letter to every major newspaper in the U.S. to declare victory.

Within three months of New Coke being introduced, the old Coke was brought back. According to some sources including Malcolm Gladwell[54], the successful taste tests of New Coke didn't ask whether consumers wanted to drink the entire 12 oz. portion, just whether a sip of the new formula was preferable

---

[54] Gladwell, M. (2005) *Blink: The Power of Thinking Without Thinking*

PART 5

HAVE THEY HEARD OF YOU?

AWARENESS EXPLAINED

Sorting the men from the boys

Getting potential customers to hear of the, by now, wonderful and relevant solutions you have developed for them, is not as easy as it used to be. The public are inundated with news bulletins, music and advertising messages every waking minute, a dizzying mix of words, graphics and sound – promotional offers, celebrity endorsements, coupons, free air miles, buy one get one free, January sales and so on. I read somewhere that the average person sees an estimated 2,000 to 3,000 adverts a day. How to get heard above the commotion? The number of channels that can provide information for a potential customer is limitless as already discussed, and all options need to be assessed, not just the usual "quick, I need to print 5,000 flyers because I want to launch my new service" approach.

You need to deliver specific information to your potential customer (which is covered in the *Information Gathering* section below), but beforehand or in tandem, you must first raise the profile of your organisation or brand, as a whole. If not, when you market more specific information it will be harder to gain initial recognition. A range of audiences, beyond your immediate community, need to get to know who you are, and quickly. You could achieve this by advertising if you had a huge budget, but better than that you can do it through media relations at little relative cost.

Awareness give a sub-conscious recognition of your company or message, so that when a potential customer subsequently sees an advert of yours, or gets a phone call from one of your sales personnel, they are more likely to be responsive because they think "I know them. I heard about them somewhere." It doesn't open doors on its own, but it allows doors to be opened more easily when you push on them.

Seth Godin a self-styled American marketing guru with a supposed cult business following, wrote a book called *Purple* Cow[55]. The title was inspired by a poem by Gelett Burgess, and seeks to show that if you want to get attention you have to be different, like a purple cow in a field of brown ones. His view was if no-one notices you, they certainly won't buy from you. As far as awareness is concerned your organisation should aim to be the purple cow of window cleaners, hotels, magazines, widget manufacturers or whatever. You should sharply and clearly highlight your differences (differentiation) from the competition and not be afraid to stand up and point out how you're unique and apart from the usual offering in your sector. This is precisely why I set up a company called Cow Marketing.

Awareness is the part of the Isaiah Logic process that takes the most intelligence and creativity. This is where the men (or women) get sorted from the boys (or girls). Because you have to work really hard on this bit; thinking it through, constantly testing and questioning it until you finally get there. I can always tell when a promotion or an ad has been dreamt up by a team of boys, as opposed to men, because the thinking is weak and intellectually thin. It's as if the marketing manager is the Emperor With No Clothes, and no-one is brave enough to question the premise, including the boss.

The worst example of lazy thinking, was the "make the husband/boyfriend look like a domestically incompetent plonker" phase in the late 1990's. Unbelievably, an occasional television advert still uses this weak theme even now. A gang of marketers obviously decided that if women buy (say) washing powder, the manufacturer could be in on the hush hush female joke that men are useless. All the ad had to do was show the man in the house in a situation where he suddenly had to cope *all on his own*. Shock, horror. Naturally, you could then see by implication that all women are far superior, and all men do nothing in the house. After all women can bring up children, cook beautifully, do the washing

---

[55] Godin, S., (2003) *Purple Cow: Transform Your Business by Being Remarkable*

standing on their heads, and be a director of an investment bank at the same time. You can just imagine the brainstorming session conducted by the bright, thrusting single young things, from redbrick universities who live in loft apartments on the outskirts of London:

"If we can show how empathetic we're, they will marvel at our articulation of the modern day working mum problem. How they'll roar with laughter at the precisely drawn useless male partner. How they're really the ones in control. Hey presto, they'll see themselves in the ad and buy the brand."

Well, it didn't work for me. My husband does all the washing in our house.

Lazily repeating what the organisation has always done or coming up with intellectually thin marketing tactics, won't make you a purple cow. You need to carefully craft what your offering is, explain why it's different and everyone (absolutely everyone) needs to buy into it at a senior level in the organisation. You must believe it and breathe it.

Getting big media profile in the *Daily Mail*, on Radio 5, BBC News, breakfast television, the *Today* programme, and so on is spectacularly easy. Honestly, it really is, as long as you have something to say, and you have a story to tell. Much better than the expense of television ads, which will be treated with a large dose of cynicism, most especially by the young, and anyhow most of us can't afford it. As long as you are brave enough to highlight your difference in approach and confident enough to commentate or contradict the issues of the day, you can do it. If you build up recognition that you are experts in just one key area (or maybe a couple), commentators will want to know what you think. Take Raymond Blanc, he may be asked by the media to speak on his knowledge of cooking, but he is more often being used as a commentator on excellent customer service. Shrewd guy – this does nothing but promote Le Manoir (his restaurant and hotel) and how important they think their customers are!

For example, the latest scares on hospital acquired infections, such as MRSA, will rumble on in the news for some time to come. Does your company specialise in cleaning services? If so, you should be giving your views on radio and television. It's pretty obvious that hospitals have cut cleaning budgets for so long, that a decent service can no longer be provided. You won't want to slam hospitals just to get airtime because they could be customers of yours, but that doesn't stop you from having the expertise to explain the issues and difficulties. That type of high profile declaration of know-how could raise awareness of your existence, especially if it were done on a reasonably regular basis. It's not necessarily specific to your individual products or services, but it is 'expertise' specific, and it would do great things for your company's morale and confidence. You could be an expert on traffic information, cheese, visitors from overseas, mobile phone systems or share dealing. The follow up of product or service specific marketing would be so much easier after that. If awareness of your organisation is raised generally, the follow up marketing activity is like pushing at an open door, rather than hammering to be let in. Your sales team will never stop thanking you.

If you feel uncomfortable with public relations or it doesn't fit your industry too well, there are dozens of other ways to gain awareness that doesn't involve big budget broadcast spend. Most of your available choices are shown in Part Four. Some cost no money at all, other may require a good sized investment. However, the key to making awareness activity work is to ensure it is closely linked to your client research (evidence-based), and the thinking is completely aligned to solving customer problems.

Synopsis

Awareness is raising your profile through advertising and promotional activity, or by highlighting expertise in key areas in which you are confident enough to commentate.

Awareness is often seen as a mass marketing activity which traditionally uses multi-million pound marketing budgets particularly in fast moving consumer goods. But it can be achieved with a smaller budget or through smart media relations activity in the public, charity, business to business or service arena, through the utilisation of internal expert commentators.

HOW TO ACHIEVE AWARENESS

Where to get the best

With your, by now, solution-based product or service portfolio and a true understanding of your customer segments, everyone needs to hear about it. If you have a marketing department, the awareness strategy must incorporate all the results of those findings – use media channels that are attractive to your existing and potential customers, and make damn sure the budget is put into areas that will give you the best return on sales, using the evidence you've gathered. Don't allow 'brainstorms' carried out in a remote location dictate strategy if there is no reference to reality.

If you want to go for pure repetition and can afford a multi-million pound campaign maybe an integrated marketing strategy including television, radio, magazine and web is appropriate. A specialised advertising agency can construct such a campaign, but make sure it is based on your findings, that your product or service is absolutely central to the communication premise and that results are tangibly measured by sales or number of enquiries. They must start here and don't allow them to come up with adverts that are just entertaining – it's not enough. You're paying, so put your foot down.

On a budget

Most organisations don't have a million pound marketing budget, so they have to think more carefully about an awareness strategy, and make every pound count towards increased sales, or whatever other objective they have set themselves. PR can achieve more coverage than paid-for advertising, so it's worth considering employing a PR company to get you into the mainstream and trade media. Often small businesses think they can do their own PR by writing a press release and sending it off themselves. This could get them into a local paper, but if you want more impact you need to buy in an agency that has media contacts and will chase them up.

When tendering for the services of a PR company[56] look for evidence that their previous campaigns have been effective in getting more sales, not just more coverage. Ask for references from their current clients, and follow them up by ringing to find out if they are happy with their services and the new business it has given them.

The minimum amount you need to pay will typically be based on a number of days per month, over the course of a fixed period. Less than three days a month will be ineffective, and a PR campaign needs to be at least six months long. Day rates are unlikely to be less than £650 a day, much more for those agencies based in London, so you need to consider if you can afford that, because anything less, just won't give you the impact you need.

For other marketing channel choices, the *Awareness Tools* section below explains each of the options in more detail, and some of these are remarkably cost effective. Where do your customers look and listen? If they use public transport, your awareness campaign needs to be seen there. If they listen to local radio in the car on the way to work, buy advertising slots on 'drive time'. If they use the web to search for your type of services invest in an agency that will help you optimise search engine results, so you're near the top. If they're Daily Star readers, don't buy space in The Daily Telegraph, it might give you status or cachet amongst your friends or shareholders, but you're wasting money.

The key decisions must be based on the findings of your insight research, so make sure the question of where your potential customer goes to be informed of new products or services, has been asked. If they have told you what media influences them most, its blindingly obvious where you need to be with your messages, all you now need to do, is look for the most cost-effective options.

---

[56] Part Four gives an example of a PR Tendering template

Where to find PR agencies

Any decent PR agency will be a member of the Chartered Institute of Public Relations (CIPR). Their website at www.cipr.co.uk, has a really useful section called "Looking for PR", which explains what you should be looking for in a PR agency. They have an agency 'matchmaking' service on the site and a facility to search for independent consultants.

Where to find advertising agencies

The Institute of Practitioners in Advertising (IPA) is the industry body and professional institute for advertising, media and marketing communications agencies in the UK. Collectively, IPA members handle over 80% of media spend in the UK and membership is through strict criteria. Their website can be found at www.ipa.co.uk. It has a search facility which allows users to find an agency by location, discipline, experience or number of employees.

Where to find SEO consultancies

For e-mail marketing, interactive advertising and search engine optimisation visit www.brandrepublic.com/revolution, which is the internet home page of *Revolution* the web industry magazine. Online they have a supplier directory where you can search for internet advertising agencies or search engine optimisation consultancies by discipline or location.

Recommended further reading

- Ogilvy, D. (2007), *Ogilvy on Advertising*
- Gurton, A. (2001), *Press Here: Managing the Media for Free Publicity*
- Laermer, R. (2004), Full Frontal PR: *Building Buzz About Your Business, Your Product, or You*
- Norman, B. (2007), *Getting Noticed on Google in Easy Steps*

If you want to know exactly how newspapers cover stories and how the editor decides what makes the front page, glance through the entertaining, but thoroughly depressing:

- Morgan, P. (2005), The Insider: *The Private Diaries of a Scandalous Decade*

AWARENESS TOOLS

When contemplating how you will achieve 'awareness', you have to make some of the most difficult decisions in the marketing process because a) there are so many options available and b) this is where the huge majority of your marketing budget will go. This is why the 'awareness' activity gains more importance over other areas of marketing, and why so many people believe advertising is marketing, when in reality it is only one step in the process.

The *Insight* and *Solution Development* activities of Isaiah Logic, should give you all the clues you need to decide on the best channels for your organisation, but as there are so many options below are some examples to help your decision making process.

Field and experiential marketing

Field marketing used to be supplied by agencies that could deliver staff for merchandising activity. Mostly they would give away product samples in-store or at public events and audit results for feedback. In essence, they were little more than short term recruitment and training agencies – think people dressed as chickens or free Baileys Irish Cream served in a thimble. However, there is now a sharp rise in 'experiential' marketing and the agencies that can deliver it. They aim to create face-to-face consumption or usage of your service or product, so that the potential customer has a favourable experience associated with your brand, and in the process can gain a deeper product/service knowledge. Essentially it is supposed to be an interactive tool which builds on "positive emotional sensory engagement"[57]. As with field marketing it is still largely used in the food and drink sector.

---

[57] or so says the Direct Marketing Association of the UK.

As an example, Absolut Vodka launched a brand called *Cut* in Australia, declining to use television advertising and using experiential marketing instead. Backed up with public relations, point-of-sale and some online advertising they leased two bars in Sydney and Melbourne, and put on DJ sets, band concerts and photo exhibitions. Visitors received a free bottle of Cut, and consumers were given a chance to contribute their photos to the exhibits, generating great word of mouth recommendation. Instead of using a mass marketing blitz to reach potential customers, they narrowly targeted fewer influential customers who would act as advocates of the brand.

These type of bespoke events are useful for product sales but could give you the opportunity to creatively explain a more complicated service and product offering. A word of warning however, if you use field staff from an agency, they are temporary representatives of your company and your brand, make sure they are high quality, well motivated and thoroughly trained on your product or service. If not, you will waste your money, and worse it will have a detrimental and adverse affect on your image, your reputation and your sales.

Guerrilla marketing

'Guerrilla Marketing' was first coined by Jay Conrad Levinson in his popular book of the same name[58]. Its original premise was how to deliver increased sales on a very low budget, by relying on time, energy and imagination instead of big marketing budgets. It is now more often used as a generic term to describe aggressive, unconventional marketing methods, and is favoured by young, hip brands wanting to make a name for themselves. Typically guerrilla marketing is now assumed to involve activities such as:

- Viral emails containing jokes or adverts
- Film making posted onto YouTube and social networking sites
- Personal canvassing and selling on the high street or at public events

---

[58] Levinson, J.C. (1984), *Guerilla Marketing*

- Use of body advertising e.g. forehead / tattoos
- Bluejacking – i.e. sending a personal message to a mobile phone via bluetooth say in a café or nightclub
- Circulars and brochures distributed at car parks, homes, offices and shopping centres
- Sabotaging of competitors' advertising such as billboards
- Use of searchlights or projectors at night
- Use of performance art / actors in the street
- Messages or adverts spray painted onto pavements or lamp posts
- Flyposting

Personally I subscribe wholeheartedly to the theory of using intelligent analysis, as the first tool to get results, however Isaiah Logic dictates that a fantastic reputation secured by word of mouth recommendation, is the ultimate objective for sustainable profit growth. Breaking the law, or irritating large swathes of the public (even if they are not your target market) may not be an ideal way of achieving that marketing nirvana. Using this approach is risky and can be illegal. It's your call.

Telemarketing

Telemarketing is a method of direct selling when a salesperson makes an unsolicited telephone call to random customers to buy products, but more usually, services. When targeting the public, such companies often use an autodialer capable of making large number of simultaneous phone calls using computer networking technology. Prospective customers are identified by various means, including past purchase history, previous requests for information, competition entry forms and application forms. Names may also be bought from another company's customer database. Generally telemarketing to your home phone is seen as a disturbing annoyance by the unwary receiver of the call. I cannot see any circumstances in which this type of marketing activity is justified, and I pity anyone who has to work in one of these call centres.

Telemarketing to businesses is slightly different, and in some way we all know that being a manager in a business, will expose us to the occupational hazard of sales calls over the phone. However, we also know that sometimes these calls will be very timely, as they may solve a current problem. If telemarketing is well-researched and polite it can be a cost-effective method for generating sales enquiries, selling products and services, but more importantly making appointments with prospective clients.

You can employ a telemarketing agency, but you need to ensure your aims, outline script, and communications process for enquiry generation follow-up, are all clearly established and understood, not only by the agency but your own staff. Do not insist on rigid scripts as they have the effect of limiting the natural style and capabilities of good telemarketing staff. Instead compile a well thought out framework to work to, so that potential customers don't find the interaction impersonal and insulting. To manage the whole process efficiently you will also need some sort of client relationship management (CRM) system to organise and manage lists, data, follow-up and outcomes.

Door-to-door marketing

Door-to-door is a sales technique in which a salesperson walks from door to door, trying to sell a product or service. It was made famous by salesmen selling the Encyclopedia Britannica and is not a tactic generally used today, although it is still beloved by politicians, councillors and Jehovah's Witness advocates. Some door-to-door catalogue sales can work well selling goods such as jewellery, tupperware or clothes, but it is seen as old-fashioned.

Outdoor and ambient media

Ambient media advertising can be used in conjunction with mainstream traditional media, or used as a stand-alone activity. It's generally considered most useful as part of a campaign so that it maintains brand awareness created by other, more mainstream and widespread, marketing efforts. Essentially it's advertising messages on everyday items that already have their own function. Often they are small in size, such as beermats. Ambient media is aimed at subtly creating brand awareness in a particularly relevant situation, and so subconsciously leading to a purchase or enforcing a message. Examples include advertising on the back of car park or supermarket receipts, advertising on pizza takeaway boxes, petrol pumps or on the handles of supermarket trolleys, etc.

Outdoor advertising also can work on its own, but is likely to be used to better effect when combined with other marketing channels such as PR. It can be effective if you want to blitz a very small area, is usually in a large format and falls into three categories:

- Billboards – generally huge poster sites of 48 or 96 sheets. Advertising sites can be bought by postcode or by demographic profiling, or through enterprising farmers that own land backing on to motorways, using old lorries as poster sites. Projections onto buildings have been used, but you need to get permission from the local council and the building owner.
- Street furniture – telephone boxes, bus shelters, litter bins, etc.
- Transit advertising – adverts at transport hubs such as the London Underground, bus stations and airports or on moving vehicles such as lorries, vans, taxis or trains.

Both outdoor and ambient media can be very cost effective when compared to national newspaper or broadcast advertising.

Events, exhibitions and festivals

Exhibitions can range from huge international trade fairs to small local exhibitions for specific industry sectors. Other events, which are becoming increasingly popular with the public are festivals centred around a theme where consumer goods can be bought on the day. The most obvious example is food or beer festivals where the event is seen as a 'day out' experience, with showcase events during the day, food and drink tastings and the opportunity to buy. A reasonably comprehensive list of exhibition and trade events held in the UK can be found at www.exhibitions.co.uk.

The most important criteria for securing an exhibition or trade stand, is to calculate the true cost of attendance. Is it worth it, once you have paid for the space and stand construction and taken into account travel and subsistence costs, along with staff time and effort? Don't forget you will also have an element of 'lost' business as your staff will not be doing their normal job if they are in attendance. If you are going solely to trade on the day, you need to carefully work out how much you will need to sell to recoup your costs, and how much you would expect to make as profit. Some organisations don't mind making a 'nominal' loss on such events, as they see it as a marketing investment, which over time will increase awareness of their company and product, or it gives them an opportunity to meet up with existing customers.

To gauge whether an exhibition will give you the return you need, ask the organisers how many people are expected, how many came last year and so on. Establish clearly whether the visitors will be the 'right' type for your company and whether they are decision makers, especially if you are selling capital equipment or a complex business service. In addition, you may want to create and advertise your own event to attract new potential customers or gain more general publicity. This could be a conference or seminar, with guest speakers and experts in your industry, and can be a good way of attracting potential customers. (See also public relations).

Sales promotion

Sales promotion is the marketing tactic employed for a pre-determined, limited time to increase consumer demand, stimulate market demand or improve product availability. Examples include competitions, money-off tokens and loyalty reward programmes. They can be aimed directly at the consumer or at sales staff or distribution channel members such as retailers. The key to these types of high profile promotions is to 'buy' custom at a low price, with a minimal profit (if any) in relation to the competition. However, the real test is to use this mechanism to increase sustainable sales, after the product or service has returned to its normal price. The way to gauge success therefore is not on the turnover of sales during the promotion, but on the sales figures and the related profit margin in the months and years after.

There are numerous ways of implementing a sales promotion including:

- Temporary reductions in price – such as *Happy Hour* or *Special Offers* or a *Sale*
- Loyalty reward programmes – where buyers collect points, miles or credits for purchases and redeem them for rewards. Examples include AirMiles and the Tesco Club Card
- Price-pack deals – where the point-of-sale or packaging offers a certain percentage extra for the same price, or Buy One Get One Free
- Money-off coupons – to encourage a second purchase at a reduced rate
- Loss leader – where a popular product or service is discounted to get buyers to make purchases on other more profitable items
- Rebates – buyers are offered money back if the receipt is mailed to the producer, often with requirement of personal information to enable them to be put on a database for future mailings
- Competitions, giveaways or prizes – involving either a series of purchases which leads to the chance of a cut-price or giveaway item, or allowing the buyer to be automatically entered into a competition or having a percentage chance of receiving a prize because of their purchase

In trade or business-to-business sales there are a number of incentives to encourage distributors or retailers to stock or buy your product or service instead of your competitors'. The most popular include:

- A short term incentive offered to induce a retailer to stock up, purchase or display a product or service.
- A competition to reward retailers that sell the most product.
- Extra sales tools or display materials given to retailers to boost sales.
- Free training programs where dealer employees are trained in selling the product or service.
- An extra commission paid to retail employees to push products.
- Trade discounts that give retailers or distribution channel members more profit from your offering, for a set period.

Point-of-sale and packaging

Point-of-sale display (often abbreviated to POS) is the form of sales promotion that draws attention to the product at the point of purchase. This is particularly pertinent to fmcg and those products that are self service, as they have to 'sell themselves', but point-of-sale promotion can also be used to highlight new products, special offers or competitions. An investment in point-of-sale materials works best if it's backed up by an awareness campaign, so that the potential consumer already has some acknowledgement of your brand, with the display triggering that recognition. Therefore point-of-sale and packaging must be consistent with the style and message of any previous awareness activity, or the link between to the two will not be made.

You can get an agency to design and build bespoke point-of-sale materials, but there are many companies that have off-the-shelf displays that can be customised with your own branding. Point-of-sale mechanisms include shelf edging, dummy packs, display packs, display stands, mobiles, posters, ticketing, leaflet dispensers, signs, shelf organisers and banners. Depending on the relationship with the retailer, some companies supply their own displays for retailers, siting, restocking and maintaining them using their own staff. This can even include the supply of vending machines, chiller cabinets or freezers. If you are responsible for displaying your product, make sure they are seen to their full potential, with the correct part of the packaging shown to the customer, with neat rows not untidy piles haphazardly placed, and that stock control is efficiently organised.

Packaging really came into its own when the advent of self-service shopping began to take hold in the 1950s. Self-service stores allowed customers to pick their own goods from the manufacturer's brands on display, rather than the shopkeeper packing them up for them. Arguably the best thing since sliced bread, was the packaging of sliced bread. The product was transformed from a generic staple to something convenient and new, that communicated freshness and portability. Mother's Pride had a waxed paper-wrapped product which was the antithesis of Hovis, the only other major bread brand. They didn't package it up at all, but instead had their name baked into the side of the loaf. Packaging has always been undervalued as a self promotion tool, and product advantage can be designed into a pack – just think of the Jif lemon packaging, or the Toilet Duck (gets under the rim of the loo), Dulux solid emulsion tailor-made for a paint roller and the toothpaste pump.

Other products that benefit from an investment in packaging design are luxury products such as perfumes and lifestyle products such as trendy new twists on alcoholic spirits. Premium pricing will only stick if the packaging reflects the perceived value and brand personality. Packaging designers will help deliver the look and form of your packaging, and should also be able to advise on materials and legal adherence. This includes information requirements, producer responsibility and environmental regulations[59].

Packaging and point-of-sale is inextricably linked with sales promotion (above), and can include the negotiations with distribution channels to 'favour' your product over the competition, especially putting it in a prominent position. Location of your product is critical, so try to agree that it is placed in 'hot spots' to capture impulse buys.

---

[59] Visit http://www.netregs.gov.uk/netregs/275207/ and scroll down to the 'packaging' link for more information.

Merchandising and giveaways

Merchandising is traditionally used by sports teams and pop groups to allow fans to show their allegiance. It is increasingly being used by film makers, publishers and mainstream brands to elicit support and to gain free advertising. It can include t-shirts, baseball caps and car stickers but is only likely to be successful if the brand is seen as stylish and aspirational. However, it can still be used by your own staff during their working operations as a form of advertising.

Business giveaways are often used during exhibitions and sales visits, as a gift for a potential or existing customer. There are hundreds of companies that can produce your logo or message on a range of sales promotion items such as pens, memory sticks, umbrellas, coasters, clocks, sticks of rock, calendars and so on. Their value as a promotional tool is debatable, as most people just want something for nothing and are unlikely to place an order just because you've given them a free biro with your name on. However, if the item is of good quality and has a real use, it can hang around your potential customers office for a long period of time, and act as a constant reminder of what your business might be able to do for them.

Corporate hospitality

Corporate hospitality has received a bad press over recent years, as unscrupulous or amateur operators have entered the industry and let down clients through inefficient organisation or not being able to get the tickets they originally promised. However, it can be a good way to cement relationships with existing clients, 'rewarding' them for staying loyal to your organisation. This gives an opportunity to spend quality time with them over a shared experience, to build trust and understand their requirements more fully. To carefully and politely look after your guests and ensure you get what you want out of the day, is a perfectly legitimate marketing tactic. Staff going along to what they see as a perk or 'jolly' and embarrassing themselves in front of clients will undoubtedly lose your business, so those attending must be well briefed and responsible.

Increasingly it is difficult to get to see decision-makers, so inviting them to an event which they would see as a privilege to attend, one way to meet and get to know them, whilst gently selling your services. If you have enthusiastic clients who can act as advocates they can help cement your new relationship, providing word of mouth recommendation and evidence of your superior service or products. Typically corporate hospitality includes attendance at sporting events, concerts, festivals, shows, the theatre or opera. Usually they are highly sought after and prestigious events where tickets are hard to obtain, such as the Wimbledon finals, the Monaco Grand Prix or a film première.

You can of course source tickets and organise the whole thing yourself, or use a corporate hospitality company who will arrange the whole package for you including travel and refreshments. Given some of the recent scandals in the industry it is best to go for a company that is listed as an "official" provider by the venue, and ensure that the correct insurances are in place. If your budget is more modest many clients appreciate a visit to the theatre or a free night out, but with litigation and changes to the law making company directors legally responsible when things go wrong, it is now best to avoid the riskier events such as abseiling, go-karting or parachuting.

Direct mail

This is the process of ordering goods by mail, and often receiving them through the mail as well. Traditional mail order is via a catalogue, typically with the addition of attractive credit terms. Because the potential consumer is not in a retail or showroom setting, this only works when they already know, or can actually 'see', what they are buying, so the catalogue or brochure needs to be filled with pictures and photographs to make it tangible. This can work well for items like wine, books and DVDs or financial services products where the buyer does not need to touch or feel the product, and already knows exactly what they're getting. It's also a useful buying mechanism for people who are housebound and do not have access to the internet, and for products which are so niche they are not available in the shops.

The key barrier is the response mechanism. If someone has to respond by writing an address on an envelope and finding a stamp, they are likely to forget or not bother, so you must make it easy for them. Provide pre-paid envelopes or a telephone ordering line, or any form of response that entails the minimum effort. Catalogue companies will often have a sales person that calls door-to-door, to mitigate the response barrier altogether, (see door-to-door marketing).

Direct mail can be targeted very tightly, using lists of existing customers or from companies who specialise in providing mailing lists of named individuals. Remember that 21% of mailings are immediately discarded unopened[60] and responses below 5% are perfectly normal, and for most companies it is less than 1%. For business to business sales, mail order may work more effectively if followed up by phone. However, don't forget that because there is so much waste associated with direct mail, you are likely to alienate customers who are environmentally aware[61].

Sales literature

This is the literature that you will need to send to, or leave with, a customer, or that they can pick up at a showroom, exhibition, event or retail space. It is used so they can gather more information about your company and its offering, or check over the details they received during your sales pitch. If the person you have been dealing with is not the final decision maker, they will use this to sell on your proposal, service or product inside their own organisation. Sales literature includes booklets, brochures, catalogues, charts, manuals, product or service information sheets, price lists or technical data in printed form, but could also be a CD-rom or DVD. In general if you have a very technical product or complex service,

---

[60] *Marketing*, 19 December 2007
[61] For key statistics and information on Direct Mail, visit the Direct Mail Information Service website at www.dmis.co.uk

which will mean a significant investment by your customer, (e.g. defence equipment), they will need large amounts of support information. Obviously if you are selling soup, it's less important.

Local advertising

Local advertising is probably covered in these other headings in one way or another, but if you offer a local service that is not too complicated to explain, you really should be doing this anyway. It costs next to nothing and it's surprising how many people it could reach. It can be used on its own or to supplement more mainstream advertising. For example supermarket boards, postcards in shop windows, leaflets distributed through doors, posters or postcards in doctors' surgeries or local shops, and of course signage or 'A' boards outside your business premises (subject to planning regulations).

Listings and internet directories

A bit like local advertising, it is silly not to put your business name and description of products or service on any free internet directories or other printed listings that are available, especially if they're free. For internet directories, test the listings for your product or service category yourself, to see how well they work and how commonly they feature in the main search engine results. Remember to use words and phrases that your potential customers would use, not technical terms only known to the industry.

Public relations

Public relations (PR) is the managing of internal and external communications, maintaining a positive image and protecting or enhancing corporate reputation. PR may involve popularising successes, downplaying failures, announcing changes, launching new products or service lines, commentating on recent events or generally raising the profile of the organisation and its staff. It is achieved not through 'paid for' awareness methods as with the other channels in this section, but by gaining exposure in the media, or through events with stakeholders, suppliers or key individuals that influence an industry sector. Information on PR agencies can be found on the Chartered Institute of Public Relations website[62].

PR activity should be measured on the media coverage generated, by working out what it would have cost to advertise on the same scale. It is generally described as equivalent advertising value, EAV or AVE. That is how PR companies claim "our campaign generated publicity worth xx thousand." You should be working on a ratio of at least 1:3 if not up to 1:10 depending on your industry sector, so that if you pay a PR agency £3,000 a month they should be generating at least £9,000 a month EAV. Don't allow agencies to measure by column centimetres, because who cares how many centimetres of coverage you've gained if no-one reads that magazine or trade paper?

Sponsorship

Sponsorship is generally taken to be the financial or material support by a company, for some independent activity (usually related to sport or the arts), not directly linked to its normal business. It's usually undertaken to develop a more favourable attitude towards the sponsoring company, so that it may be seen as a caring employer, good corporate citizen, a part of the local community and so on. It is particularly useful for organisations that do not feel advertising will help their perception in the public eye, and so a more subtle form of reputation management is required. For example, BNFL who owns Sellafield and other nuclear decommissioning plants, does not want to advertise its work too prominently to the public, however it supports small sports clubs and other charitable ventures to quietly build its local reputation.

Increasing sums of money are being spent on sponsorship and with the 2012 Olympics coming to London, it is likely to gain even more credence as an awareness medium in its own right. The best

---

[62] www.cipr.co.uk

forms of sponsorship are those that reach your target market base, so if you have customers who are mad football fans, it's not very helpful to support the English National Ballet. However, an up and coming team in the vicinity may really benefit from your support, and you could gain huge 'brownie' points from your current and potential customers.

Traditionally, it's been used not so much for altruistic reasons but for more specific objectives. For example, with the ban on tv advertising of cigarettes, manufacturers maintained their television presence through sports sponsorship such as cricket's Benson and Hedges Cup. Sponsorship should only be used if it fits with the objectives and the culture of the organisation, as the public, and therefore potential buyers, can smell superficial or cynical attempts to ingratiate, from a million miles away.

Endorsements and testimonials

Using endorsements or testimonials is nothing new. Usually they are a written or spoken statement from a customer, sometimes from a famous person, extolling the virtues of your product or service, or backing a public campaign. Testimonials were used commonly in the advertising of the 19th and early 20th century, often in relation to the miracle powers of medicines or cosmetics. The makers of *Vin Mariani*, a patent medicine, secured one of the most valuable testimonials ever by receiving the recommendation of the Pope. There is also of course, the famous "by appointment to" when a monarch gives a royal endorsement. Endorsements can work well if you can get a genuine quote from a valued customer who is respected in your sector. In the professional services industry, using client case studies to highlight successes shows your experience, and is especially valuable if the client is a blue chip company or household name.

It pains me to say it, as often they're so difficult to work with, but celebrities can give you an edge when it comes to an awareness campaign. Let's face it, if you used your next door neighbour to endorse your window cleaning business, they wouldn't gain as much coverage or interest as Victoria Beckham. When a celebrity endorses your company their own image and reputation are at stake, so it implies that you're reputable and reliable.

You could use a celebrity for endorsement, to appear in publicity materials, at a launch event, to speak at a conference or to give a written testimonial. It's almost impossible to contact a celebrity direct so you either need to find the name of their agent, (usually these are even worse to deal with than the celebrity themselves), or a celebrity speaker company of which there are many (just search the internet). If you want to use your local newsreader you may be able to secure them for as little as £2,000 for a couple of hours, but if it's anybody that most people have heard of, you need to allocate between £10,000 and £25,000 from your marketing budget. If it's somebody that everyone has heard of, even your great aunt, £50,000 is nearer the mark. Obviously if you want to secure their involvement for a year for a running campaign this could cost £250,000. Tiger Woods signed a deal with Nike for $100 million a year, but you're budget probably isn't in that league.

However, such huge amounts can be worth it. George Foreman was signed up by Salton in 1994, to endorse their Lean Mean Fat Reducing Grilling Machine. By 1999, the ex-boxer had become so integral to the success of the company, that they signed a five year deal with him worth $137.5 million.[63] Sainsbury's use of Jamie Oliver has been instrumental in turning their fortunes around, after they lost ground to the other supermarkets in the late 1990s. The deal he signed was worth £1.2 million a year, but the adverts in which he featured saw a huge increase in sales for the products that were endorsed. For example, sales of a Balti sauce increased by 1040% over a four week period. Since 2000, the Jamie Oliver campaign has delivered £1.12 billion in incremental value and a return on investment of £27.25 for every advertising pound spent.[64]

If you don't know which celebrity to use or who's available, the celebrity speaker company will take a brief from you and recommend who to use given the budget at your disposal. Always

---

[63] Pringle, H. (2004), *Celebrity Sells*
[64] Ibid

negotiate, and if you're a charity try and pull at the heartstrings to get a serious discount. If you want to keep up to date with celebrity newsworthiness (and thereby their marketing value) visit www.bbc.co.uk/celebdaq. This is the site of a celebrity stock exchange game. Instead of shares in companies, shares in celebrities are traded. Their value is calculated by how much press coverage they have received that week, which will give you an excellent feel for who is creating the most interest. Alternatively, try and bring yourself to read *Hello* or *Heat* magazine.

Product placement

Product placement began in the 1940s but has really become big business in the last ten years or so. Product placement companies can approach producers of plays, films, television series, music videos, video games and books to feature your product or give it a favourable mention. This is done under the premise that your product is a (supposedly) natural part of the backdrop or script. Most major television series and film releases today contain product placements. These are negotiated either with a fee involved or in return for the provision of free props. Cisco Systems used a product placement company, 1st Place, to get their phone systems on to prime time television slots. They worked not only to get the phones seen on-screen, but install the phones to be fully functional so they are used as part of the action. Spooks, Rebus, Silent Witness and Waking the Dead are just some of the productions featuring Cisco phones.

But the really big budgets for product placement are reserved for blockbuster films as they are not only seen on release, but on DVD and television, sometimes for decades afterwards. A recent film to be heavily criticised for product placement was the James Bond film *Casino Royale* featuring Daniel Craig. Eon the production company negotiated deals with six key brands – Sony Ericsson phones, Sony Electronics, Omega watches, Heineken beer, Smirnoff vodka and Ford – including, of course, its Aston Martin badge. There were also a handful of other associated brands such as Turnbull & Asser,

Bollinger and Virgin. In one scene the love interest Vesper Lynd looks at Bond's wrist and says: "Beautiful watch. Rolex?" He replies "No, Omega."

There are rumours that the income from product placement was around £40 million, with Ford alone paying £15 million. However, not all deals are for product placement. Smirnoff Vodka used their advertising contacts and experience to promote the film during its first week, essentially paying for launch week publicity for the film company. Some products are so costly that film producers are happy to use them free of charge. Why pay for an expensive supercar that will be wrecked in a car chase, if a manufacturer will supply one free of charge? With more and more people using Sky Plus and skipping adverts, product placement is likely to increase in popularity as an awareness channel, and it does work. When **Tom Cruise** wore a pair of 1952 Ray-Ban 'Wayfarers' in the film *Risky Business*, sales increased from 18,000 to 260,000 in that same year.

Customer publishing

Customer publishing is the publication of your own book or magazine specifically for your customers. Sainsbury's magazine is an example. It was launched in 1993, claims to have a readership of 3 million and is published monthly. It features money-off coupons as well as recipes and features on lifestyle, food, in-store products and producer profiles. Manchester United has its own magazine as does Sky, Harley-Davidson, Bang & Olufsen, Waterstones, Marks & Spencer, most of the banks and car manufacturers, and of course, the airlines and train operating companies, (you've got to read something when you're delayed a couple of hours).

The customer publishing industry is worth more than £385m a year, and it is claimed that on average you will gain an 8% increase in sales by having one, and your customers on average will spend **25 minutes reading it**[65]. Naturally, this depends on the quality of the magazine and whether the articles are interesting or relevant to the

---

[65] Research by Millward Brown, for the Association of Publishing Agencies. See www.apa.co.uk

reader. If you cannot afford the cost of an in-house magazine, you can still produce newsletters or guide books. Newsletters need to contain interesting information, otherwise it will not get read and go straight in the recycling bin. Treat it as if it is a mini-magazine, not a long diatribe about your products or services, endless pages of people shaking hands receiving prizes or teams of your staff having their photo taken.

Guides can also be an interesting form of self-promotion, giving your suppliers or customers information on how to master a difficult industry problem or process, or giving hints and tips on particular subjects. For example, many accountancy firms publish guides to the latest budget from the Chancellor of the Exchequer, explaining complex tax changes and the ways to maximise tax-free income. The advantage is, if they are really useful, they will have a long shelf-life and remain on desks and in bookcases for a considerable time.

Newspaper advertising

National newspaper advertising is an expensive affair, with a full page in colour costing up to £55,000. The nation's most popular daily rag (The Sun) has an audited readership of just over 8 million, with sales of 3 million copies every weekday. In general, the higher the readership the more the cost of advertising, but newspapers such as the Financial Times or Daily Telegraph can charge more of a premium because of the buying power of their readers.

To place an advertisement in any newspaper you need to ask for their media pack or 'rate card', or sometimes they're called 'crib sheets'. This should give, not only full details of costs in the main newspaper or any supplements, but also its audited circulation figures and the demographic profile of their readers. It allows advertisers to profile readers and see if they match their target market and also to place adverts next to relevant sections such as sports reports, television schedules or lifestyle articles. The rate card charges for most of the daily newspapers can be found at www.nmauk.co.uk[66]. There are a handful of key regional newspapers that are not quite as expensive but do have a large readership, including The Evening Standard (London), Manchester Evening News and The Birmingham Post. These are often sold from lunchtime or early evening to catch commuters on their journey home.

Local newspapers are usually free and delivered through residents' letterboxes. They can have a surprisingly high readership, although it is difficult to gain real information as the figures are based on distribution rather than the actual number of readers. They are under pressure from online news media which is taking market share, but are still popular with older readers. You do have the advantage of selecting a small geographical target market and this can be a good option if you are advertising a business that operates locally. The rates are a lot lower than national newspapers, with advertising rates costing just a couple of hundred pounds.

There is quite a lot of evidence to suggest that the public are less sceptical about the reliability of the editorial in local, rather than national papers, but whether that translates to their thoughts on advertising content is not known. If you intend using newspaper advertising consistently over time, it may be worth subscribing to BRAD[67] Insight, which gives details of all local, regional and national newspaper data (around 13,500 entries), but it does cost well over £1,000 a year[68]. However, you can get access to hard copies of BRAD or Willings Press Guide at your local library. If you just want readership data, this can be found at www.jicreg.co.uk free of charge, but you will need to register. Always remember that the quoted rate for advertising space is only the starting point – try to negotiate discounts or better positioning.

One of the advantages of the newspaper medium is it enables you to send in the copy and have it displayed in the section you want within a few days, so the advert can be relatively topical, (say, relating to a sporting event, political announcement, etc.).

[66] The website of the Newspaper Marketing Agency.
[67] British Rate and Data
[68] www.bradinsight.com

Whichever newspaper you use, always remember it's a format that has a very short shelf life, it literally will be recycled or used to wrap fish and chips the very next day, (I know they're not allowed to do that anymore, but you know what I mean). In addition, there are the new free daily newspapers such as The Metro. This was launched in 1999, has 13 regional editions and a combined readership of around 1.3 million.

Magazine advertising

Much of the information on newspaper advertising (above) is relevant to magazine advertising, however the lead time to get your advert published can be three to six weeks. There are two types – lifestyle/consumer magazines and trade/technical press. The first are publications generally sold or made available to the public either through your letterbox, given away on the street or bought at retail outlets. The latter are technical and professional magazines read by customers, suppliers and businesses in a particular sector. Some are sold via subscription or in retail outlets and others are free, but usually only after you have submitted comprehensive details about yourself or your business.

Magazines provide a variety of ways to advertise:

- Classified advertising – particularly for small ads
- Display advertising – a traditional large advert from a quarter of a page upwards, the full page or double page spreads being more sophisticated, often appearing on editorial pages or in special supplements
- Advertisement features – they're designed to look a bit like an editorial page but feature you and your business or product. You pay for them, and the magazine may also throw in some other advertising space. Your suppliers might advertise around the feature thus offsetting the cost
- Loose inserts – you design, print and supply these to the magazine publisher for them to insert into the magazine

You can get information on many publishers and magazines on the

Periodical Publishers Association website at www.ppa.co.uk. As mentioned above, BRAD or Willings Press Guide will give you indicative costs.

Media buying

Media buying is the term to describe the purchase of advertising space in magazines, newspapers or on the web, or advertising time on television, cinema or radio. If you have done some background research on the readership or listener profile of a particular magazine, newspaper or radio station, you can ring them up direct and negotiate your own deal. There is no need to involve an intermediary as the process is relatively simple, however if you were going to plan a heavy weight campaign across a number of titles, or a range of radio stations, it may be worth involving a media buying agency as they could negotiate substantial discounts for you.

These agencies can achieve discounts based on the total volume of advertising they buy on behalf of all their clients. They have far more buying power than you do as an individual company. You may also want to use an agency if you don't want to conduct the readership profile research, as described earlier. You give the media buying agency an outline of your target customers and where they operate, and they can recommend which media to use. They will either charge a fee, or take commission on the amount of advertising you intend to purchase, or both.

Online media buying is a new marketing discipline, and as internet advertising is still in its infancy it is in a constant state of flux. New and innovative interactive options are constantly being introduced such as geographically and behaviourally-targeted advertising. Online media buying requires in-depth knowledge and it is probably best to use an experienced agency to recommend not only a media buying plan, but a complete strategy.

If you want to plan a television or cinema advertising campaign, you really will need to use a media buyer, mainly because the key players have immense buying power but also they understand its complexities. Television time especially, is incredibly complicated to buy and uses intricate formulas, not only to calculate costs, but the number of viewers who will see your ad, and how likely they are to be your key target audience. This is based on the profile of the audience that watches particular programmes or channels, either on terrestrial or satellite television. As an advertiser you will be given details of 'reach' and 'frequency'.

Reach is how many of your targeted audience have an 'opportunity to see' (OTS) your ad. They use the term OTS because although a programme such as Desperate Housewives may have a viewing audience of x million, some of them will have gone to the loo or made a cup of tea during the commercial break. So they don't actually see your ad, but they have the opportunity to do so. Frequency is how often you want your ad played. A big decision is whether to go for a burst over a small timeframe covering a wide audience or stick to certain programmes which you know your target audience watch, and keep delivering the ad to that niche audience over a longer period. This will, of course, depend on the nature of your product or service offering, and the media buying agency can give you advice.

The first time you get a media schedule from an agency, you will see all the key programmes that are associated with your target audience, however there will be slots for your advertising at 3am on a Wednesday, and you will wonder what you're paying for. No-one in their right mind would choose that as their premium spot, so when you buy packages, it will be filled not only with the times and programmes that you want, but a selection of 'fillers' for rarely viewed programmes too. It's all part of the total package you will need to buy.

Cinema advertising works in a number of ways, and again it is best to use a media buying agency as they will be able to get a better deal from the key advertisers such as Carlton Screen Advertising or Pearl & Dean. If you have a well defined target audience, it is probably best to buy packages that precede specific films. These will also have well drawn profiles of the intended target audience and you can match them up. For example, if you are selling magic tricks for children, it would make sense to buy a package around the latest Harry Potter film. Alternatively, if you want to advertise locally you can nominate individual screens or venues to show your advert.

Television and cinema advertising

Television advertising revenue continues to fall, but it is still regarded as the most glamorous of marketing mediums, although unfortunately not always the most effective, which can make it a very expensive mistake. Conversely, cinema advertising has been increasing as more films are being produced, and visiting the cinema has increased in popularity. If you use either medium, the advert has to get results i.e. sell the product or service. Creating general awareness is fine if you have a huge marketing budget, and this is just part of a complex marketing strategy using a range of mediums. But the overall aim of any marketing campaign, is that eventually it leads to a sustainable increase in sales or take-up, this is the only measure that counts.

Marketing magazines and advertising agencies often measure effectiveness on 'recall'. That is to say, they go out on the street and ask the general public which adverts they have remembered from the previous week. I cannot unearth any robust evidence to prove that recall equals a purchase. David Ogilvy, who started one of the most famous advertising agencies in the world – Ogilvy and Mather (now part of WPP), wrote that he prefers measures on changes to brand preference because . . .

"people who register a change in brand preference after seeing a commercial subsequently buy the product three times more than people who don't. Research organizations also measure the recall of commercials, and this method finds favour with many advertisers. But some kinds of television commercials which get high recall scores get low scores on changing brand preference, and there appears to be no correlation between recall and purchasing."[69]

---

[69] Ogilvy, D. (1983), *Ogilvy on Advertising*

Brand preference measures are an improvement on recall, but still not the most important measure. I might see a wonderful car ad which changes my preference to Ferrari as a brand instead of Porsche, but I can't afford one, so who cares?

If your insight research tells you that television is the best medium to reach your target audience, use a well respected agency to produce your advert. However, when holding a beauty parade on potential candidates, insist on credentials that have measured their past record on increasing sales, not establishing brand preference, winning awards or gaining recall. A well produced, intelligent television advert could make a huge positive impact on your business or on a public campaign, but it will cost a lot of money so make sure it's more than just memorable. It just produces hard results.

Radio advertising

Radio advertising can be a viable option even for those companies on a tight budget. Local radio stations can attract a loyal following and small businesses in particular can benefit from the close relationship between some commercial stations and their listeners. As with most broadcast and print advertising, the cost will depend on the listener numbers, so as always you need to match the radio station's audience profile to your intended target audience. Unlike television and cinema advertising where you need to hire an agency to produce your advert, radio stations will usually produce your advert for you. Generally the quality is reasonable, but if you plan a big campaign across a number of stations it may be best to get in a specialised agency, to come up with a creative script and produce it for you. Most radio stations are flexible about your advertising options, rather than a repeated advert you could sponsor particular shows or features, or run a competition on air.

If you go direct to the radio station you need to consider the length of the advert ranging from ten seconds to over a minute, although thirty seconds is standard. The time of day, or what programme the advert will be in, should be dependent on your intended audience. If they are likely to be driving to work, then go for drive time in the morning or evening (more expensive), but if it is aimed at people at home or working in a factory or office setting where the radio is playing, avoid lunchtimes, but go for mid-morning or mid-afternoons. You also need to consider frequency and length.

The radio station will charge you for creating the advert, but that should cost a maximum of 10% of the overall cost. This includes script writing, voiceovers, music and sound effects. In addition, there is usually an option to advertise on the station's website, which is generally very cost effective, and would be particularly useful if you were running a competition linked to your advert. To find out about the available radio stations and the latest facts and figures on radio audiences, visit the Radio Advertising Bureau[70].

Podcasting

There is a way in which you can do your own pseudo-radio advertising through your website. Podcast is a term which is a combination of the words i-pod and broadcast. Basically it's a way of posting an audio file on the internet, which can be downloaded by others and saved on a portable media player or computer, for later listening. Any web agency can set these up for you, and it has been used to great effect by the BBC for radio programmes. However, no-one is likely to download a pure advert so it would need to be highly entertaining. Cobra Beer launched a series of pub-based podcasts in June 2008, hosted by Xfm radio DJ Danny Wallace and comedian Dom Joly. It comprised ten 15-minute episodes of unscripted banter between the hosts and their guests, and was released fortnightly through Cobra's website.

You could also place podcasts of any radio adverts you have commissioned on your website. At least it will make the most of your marketing spend, with the advert outlasting your mainstream media campaign.

---

[70] www.rab.co.uk, but you will need to register.

Blogging

Blogging is a way of sharing your thoughts and ideas with people online. Blogs (or web logs) are basically online journals or diaries which are great for sharing information and ideas or your own private thoughts. Some people use them as a political soapbox. As well as text, blogs often contain audio, music, images and video. Generally, they are uploaded by individual members of the public, but organisations can also benefit. They're really easy and cheap to do, so if you feel that a particular person from your company (whether a figurehead or perhaps a fictional character), can create a following on the web which will enhance your company reputation or get publicity for your brand, it's worth considering.

If you cannot afford the services of a web company and don't have the technical skills, you can create a blog, using a hosted blog service. Essentially, they 'host' your blog at their domain. They make creating a blog easy by providing well-designed templates, a web address and rich text editors that allow you to create posts without any special technical knowledge. It's easy to have a blog, up and running in less than ten minutes and some of the hosting services are provided free (just one example is wordpress.com).

Don't forget that there have been a number of court cases involving blogging, including issues of deformation and liability, and some employees have even lost their jobs by being too frank about their employer. In 2003, a college lecturer was found guilty of referring to a politician as a "nazi". Even though she used a pseudonym, her identity was discovered through her internet service provider and she was successfully sued by the politician, who was awarded £10,000 in damages and £7,200 costs.[71] You also need to be careful not to reveal company confidential information or information about client details, including the provisions of the Data Protection Act.

---

[71] *The Guardian*, 23 March 2006.

Digital and search engine advertising

Digital advertising is a new awareness medium, but is fast becoming more important, and some would argue, more effective than traditional forms of advertising such as television and newspapers. As explained in the media buying section above, it is a rapidly developing technology so you are best using an agency who can guide you through the choices available. In essence though the main options are:

Text

Advertisements displayed as simple, text-based hyperlinks that usually direct users to your website and do not include graphic images. Text ads are generally sold on non-search websites by companies who have high traffic. Often they want to make extra money out of their site or provide their customers with pointers to a range of other services so it becomes a portal in its own right i.e. where you go if you want to know anything to do with their market, not just their product or service portfolio.

Display

Display ads are largely the same as above, but are available in a range of standard shapes and sizes, and use eye-catching visuals to attract attention.

Pop-Ups

These are the advertisements that appear to 'pop up' in a new window as users browse a website. Hover, floating and slide-in adverts are all considered pop-ups. These are often seen as obtrusive and irritating, and many systems now have blockers to stop these from arriving on your desktop. You will need to think carefully about your company reputation if you want to use this form of advertising.

Flash/DHTML

These incorporate Flash animation or other motion graphics. They can be animated display adverts in traditional shapes and sizes, or have a more sophisticated function similar to pop-up ads but with much deeper integration into the overall design of the site.

Interstitial

Interstitial adverts appear when the user is waiting for a web page to download. In this context, interstitial is used to mean "in between". The interstitial web page sits between a referenced page and the page which references it, hence it's in between two pages. This is distinct from a page which simply links directly to another. For example, if you have read a snippet of an online news story and click to read the whole article, an interstitial advert could appear while you are waiting for the new page to download. Typically then, these adverts will last five to ten seconds, and load in the background so that they do not interrupt the intended page download. Most advertisers who use this method, do so because it enables them to use rich media, streaming video, and/or large graphics, an option that is not often open to them in other forms of digital advertising. However it is an intrusion, and needs to be weighed up in terms of company reputation.

Video

With the popularity of online video watching, these have become a viable means of distributing rich advertising content. Currently video adverts can be stand alone, or can be placed within a longer video, a bit like a television commercial during a programme. Major search engines such as Google, MSN, Yahoo! and AOL all offer advertising on their video websites.

E-mail

There are two types of e-mail adverts – classified or newsletters. The first are blatant 'classified' adverts sent out via e-mail. These can be stand alone, or be bought as part of another organisation's wider e-mail content such as a newsletter. Airlines for example, will often do this to advertise cut-price flight offers. Usually you opt in, by registering or clicking a box to agree to receive these mailings when you have made a purchase. E-newsletters or e-zines are a more subtle way of advertising your business, not by using an obvious advert, but by providing news, gossip or other content that may be of interest to potential and existing clients, influencers and stakeholders. They are effective at keeping your company 'top of mind' over a long period, but make sure it is easy to 'unsubscribe'.

On-site sponsorships

On-site sponsorships are adverts (typically just a company's logo) that can be bought on individual websites. These typically appear in an area on the website reserved for sponsors and often noted as such.

Advertorials

These are advertisements in editorial form that appear to contain objectively-written opinions. Known as 'advertorials', they are used mostly in magazine advertising. Online advertorials are typically featured on a main contractor's website and promotes products and services related to the website's content. For example, a tool manufacturer may wish to promote a contract they have fulfilled, and place some of the other suppliers around the case study. These suppliers pay for those 'adverts' and so the manufacturer generates income, or adds more depth and value to their sales message.

Adwords and sponsored search

Probably the best known way to advertise on the internet, you create a textual advert and then select words or phrases that are related to your business. For example, "cheap flights", "airfares", "flight offers" or "airline tickets". When someone goes online and conducts an internet search using one of your key words, your advert appears next to the search results. Typically you only pay when the user clicks on your advert and goes through to your website, (pay per click), not every time it appears. There is often an option to set a daily budget (say £5 per day), so once your advert has been 'clicked on', the required number of times, it doesn't appear again until the next day, and you never go over your budget limit. This form of advertising is available on all the major search engine sites such as Google, MSN, Yahoo! and AOL.

Contextual targeting

When online adverts appear which are related to the content you are viewing, it is known as contextual targeting. For example, if you are reading an article on a news website about football, you may see contextual ads next to it for sports equipment, memorabilia, or tickets. Contextual adverts are purchased through the major search engines. Relevancy is typically determined by algorithms that will assess the appropriateness of the advert in relation to the displayed content, so if there is an article on rugby, an advert selling rugby shirts will appear above an advert selling football shirts.

Behavioural targeting

This is the same as contextual targeting, except it is based on the users past search and purchase history, not on subject topics. Behavioural targeting is based on a variety of online factors like recent purchases, searches, and browsing history, as well as demographic details such age or gender. For example, if you recently visited an estate agents website, you may see behavioural adverts selling mortgages next to a web section you are browsing.

Geo-targeting

Again, similar to contextual and behavioural targeting, except that this is for advertisers interested in targeting users within a specific locality or region.

Viral campaigns

There is some debate over the definition of a viral campaign. Originally it was a term that described electronic communication only, but increasingly it is being used as a generic term to describe the word of mouth recommendation process. Among the first to write about viral marketing on the internet was Douglas Rushkoff[72], he believed that if a message was absorbed and believed by a "susceptible" user, that user would become "infected" and would then go on to infect other susceptible users, spreading the message or virus through the internet or e-mail. If highly successful the message could grow almost exponentially over a very short period.

This theory was soon taken up by marketers who realised that if they could identify people with naturally large social networks, they could be intentionally targeted and used as the start of a viral campaign. On the internet, social networking sites such as FaceBook and MySpace, and video sharing sites such as YouTube are hubs for viral campaigns[73]. Experiential marketing (see above) also uses the theory to bring products and services to key influencers in social networks.

Word of mouth reputation is a central theme to this book, and probably the only real measure of product or service excellence, and overall company reputation. It is unlikely that a viral campaign can be successful if the offering is substandard or average, or lacks originality and creativity in the face of stiff competition. I don't believe that viral campaigns or viral marketing is a separate marketing discipline in its own right, it is the ultimate aim of any of the awareness channels you choose to use.

---

[72] Rushkoff, D. (1994), *Media Virus!: Hidden Agendas in Popular Culture*
[73] See case studies on OK Go, Cadbury's Gorilla and Teen Road Safety.

OTHER THINGS TO CONSIDER

Statutory control of radio and television advertising

Regulation of television and radio advertising is under the control of the Independent Television Commission (ITC) and the Radio Authority. For television, the Code of Advertising Standards and Practice states the General Principle that television advertising should be "legal, decent, honest and truthful". It is set out in a range of rules and appendices with more detailed standards relating to advertising and children, financial advertising, medicines, treatments, health claims, nutrition and dietary supplements, charity advertising and religious advertising. The Broadcasting Act 1990 and 1996[74] contains provisions which relate to the times when adverts may appear, and on their frequency and duration. Adverts are excluded from some types of programmes such as religious services, royal ceremonies or occasions, and those broadcast for reception at schools.

If you use an agency to produce a television advert, it is mandatory to clear it before it's broadcast. Clearance is given or withheld by a Copy Clearance Secretariat operated on behalf of the ITC by the Broadcast Advertising Clearance Centre (BACC). This office scrutinises tens of thousands of scripts every year. In practice, advertisers not only submit scripts but various other prototypes of the commercial for approval, because they don't want to incur expensive costs to change the finished product. If an advert is fully produced and is rejected, it is very unlikely to ever get any airtime, as individual television stations that play uncleared commercials can jeopardise their broadcasting franchise. The ITC also has a statutory responsibility to invite and investigate complaints from the viewing public about commercials which have successfully cleared the system.

---

[74] More information at www.ofcom.org.uk

The Radio Authority has a separate Advertising and Sponsorship Code, which contains the same principles. It states that "editorial control of sponsored programmes must remain with the licensee" (the radio station) and that "all sponsor involvement must be declared so that the listener knows who is paying/contributing and why." If a commercial will only be played locally it must be pre-cleared by the individual radio station, which is held responsible for "ensuring that any advertising and sponsorship they broadcast complies with this Code". However, commercials to be aired nationally or regionally must be submitted to the Radio Advertising Clearance Centre. If listeners complain about commercials which have survived local clearance, it is the station's responsibility to "adopt appropriate procedures" and to refer any unresolved complaints to the Radio Authority. Any station which receives public complaints runs the risk of having its franchise revoked or could face a hefty fine.

Control of cinema advertising combines some statutory control with an element of self-regulation. In general, cinema commercials are subject to the ASA's Code (see below), but the process is the same as television as they must be cleared by the Cinema Advertising Association's Copy Panel, before prints are distributed to cinemas. All commercials of 30 seconds or longer must secure a certificate from the British Board of Film Classification, to ensure, for example, that an 18 rated advert is not seen alongside a U classified children's film.

Self-regulated control of advertising

The Advertising Standards Authority (ASA) controls the self-regulation of non-broadcast advertising such as any form of printed advertising, or adverts through other mediums such as the internet or CD-roms. The ASA is financed by a 0.1% levy on the cost of every display advert placed in all non-broadcast media, and works to the British Code of Advertising, Sales Promotion and Direct Marketing. It is often referred to as the CAP code and has the same general principles as for broadcasting i.e. that they should be "legal, decent, honest and truthful". There are no formal requirements for pre-clearance, but if any advertiser feels they are sailing close to the wind, they can refer them for pre-checking. The public have a good overall awareness of the ASA and its role, and are encouraged to submit complaints.

When a complaint is submitted it goes through an adjudication process. If there are sufficient grounds for the complaint, the ASA can ask advertisers to withdraw or modify their advert, (admittedly this is after it has appeared). They detail their judgements in reports to the media and other interested parties, with the real possibility that transgressors of the Code will receive negative publicity. If there is no response, the media (whose trade bodies are signatories to the Code) are asked to deny space to the advertiser in future and refuse commission to the advertising agency involved. The ASA can also refer the organisation to the Office of Fair Trading if they feel that there are any legal transgressions.

Recommended further reading

The Trading Standards website at www.tradingstandards.gov.uk has a number of guidance leaflets for businesses, including one on the Trades Descriptions Act. The Office of Fair Trading also has a website at www.oft.gov.uk, where you can download a business guide on the Consumer Protection from Unfair Trading Regulations. Full details of the British Code of Advertising, Sales Promotion and Direct Marketing, the Code of Advertising Standards and Practice and the Advertising and Sponsorship Code can be found at www.asa.org.uk/asa/codes.

THAT'S THE WAY TO DO IT

Real life awareness examples

Cadbury's Dairy Milk – "gorilla"

In 2007, Cadbury's released a new television campaign featuring a Gorilla playing the drums to a Phil Collins hit. The aim was to attract a younger consumer to Dairy Milk, alongside Crunchie and Flake. The £6.2 million campaign centred around the advert directed by Juan Cabral of the advertising agency Fallon London, and become a huge internet hit. It had seven million viewings on YouTube, and users of the video-sharing website have made about 100 spoofs.

The hairy gorilla was made by Stan Winston Studios who have created 'suits' for classic action films such as The Terminator, Aliens and Edward Scissor Hands. It reputedly cost £100,000. The actor in the suit, Garon Michael, appeared in *Congo* and *Planet of the Apes*. He has reputedly spent a lifetime perfecting his gorilla art with visits to observe the animals in their natural habitat, on film and in zoos.

Prior to the campaign Dairy Milk held 9% of the total confectionery market share, with annual sales of more than £360 million. By the end of October 2007 sales were up 9% year on year during the period the advert was on air. In terms of recognition, the link with the Gorilla ad and the brand gained the highest recognition amongst consumers ever recorded.

THAT'S THE WAY TO DO IT

Real life awareness examples

OK Go – "here it goes again"

The music industry is struggling to overcome the advent of the internet and digital downloads, but savvy bands are using it to their advantage. The traditional business model, where CDs were marketed using videos shown on TV music programmes, directed by Hollywood film directors costing thousands of pounds, used to guarantee sales but now no longer works.

Chicago rock band OK Go had released a couple of albums, and had their videos shown on MTV, however a video made by themselves and posted on YouTube has made them internationally popular and increased CD sales. Choreographed by the sister of a member of the band, their 'treadmill' video has been viewed over 32 million times on the Internet and featured on news programmes globally.

OK Go's experience shows that web users can catapult a band to fame, without the usual huge marketing budget. Music distribution and accompanying videos are firmly digital, with fans downloading and viewing via the internet and on MP3 players or iPods. Sites such as YouTube, MySpace, PureVolume and others allow aspiring artists to post videos, usually grainy lo-fi productions, at little or no cost.

"Here it goes again" was supposedly made in just five takes, and is not only one of the most-viewed videos on YouTube but also one of the most imitated.

THAT'S THE WAY TO DO IT

Real life awareness examples

Department of Transport – "teen road safety"

In 2003 more than 1,400 teenagers were seriously injured or killed on the roads. However, teenagers think they know how to cross the road and don't want to be lectured about road safety, with only 4% rating it as a major concern. The marketing challenge was to find a way to get into their lives and make a connection to get the road safety message across. A range of media was used with viral internet marketing at the core. To bring the consequences of not paying attention to life, and to make it more real and applicable to teenagers it was filmed entirely on a mobile phone. This gave the advert more immediacy and intimacy, and made it look as if an accident had been filmed by one of a group of friends.

Teenagers were given phones and asked to film genuine road-side behaviour and this was used for the first twenty seconds of the advert. The final ten seconds showed the chilling conclusion giving the Department of Transport a totally authentic film that could speak to teens in their own language. The advert was launched virally on a bespoke website – www.notlooking.co.uk – and for the first week it was shown unbranded to make it more likely to be forwarded.

After a week online, the ad was shown on television in the first episode of the (then) new series of X-Factor on ITV 1 before using Channel 4 and satellite stations. It was shown in three bursts, in August 2005, January 2006 and March 2006 and in cinemas alongside teen films such as Doom and Final Destination 3. Other media activity included print and bus stop advertising located close to secondary schools.

There was substantial coverage of the new advert on the major news channels and papers as a news item in itself. 52%

of the targeted age group spontaneously recalled the advert without prompting. Nine out of ten said it made them think again about being careful on the roads (92%) or made them realise it could happen to them (90%). There has also been activity in teen chat rooms (for example there was discussion in the Celebrity Big Brother chat room), with thought and discussion about road safety issues and many debating whether the commercial was 'real'.

THAT'S THE WAY TO DO IT

Real life awareness examples

Asthma UK – "asthma attack card"

With a limited budget Asthma UK turned to television advertising to recruit donors and to change attitudes about the condition. Research showed that although the condition was widespread with over five million sufferers, asthma was regarded as a common but not serious condition. Despite the fact that 1,400 people die every year from asthma in the UK and 90% of these deaths are preventable, this widespread perception was a major barrier to attracting donations. The research also indicated that only people with asthma, their families or carers were likely to become donors.

A concentrated week of television promotion was planned, promoting the Asthma Attack Card, which was designed to be carried in a wallet or purse and explained what to do in the event of an attack. Focusing on a single week also enabled PR activity to work alongside the television airings, with specialist nurses and supporters on stand-by for media interviews. The free card helped highlight the seriousness of the condition, encouraged sufferers to identify themselves and also demonstrated the charity's value. A voice-over at the end of the advert explained how to order the card while the on screen message summed up the campaign: "Don't under-estimate asthma, it's a fatal mistake."

The charity answered more than 26,000 calls in response to the campaign, 60% above target, and each caller was offered a card. In total nearly 47,000 cards were distributed and 90% of callers agreed to receive further communications. Nearly 2,300 became new cash donors over the telephone, up 17% on campaign targets.

THAT'S THE WAY TO DO IT

Real life awareness examples

The Body Shop

In 1976, Anita Roddick opened the first Body Shop in Brighton, selling vegetable-based products ranging from Body Butter to Peppermint Foot Lotion. Roddick paid a student £20 to design the original logo and labels for the products and encouraged customers to bring back packaging so it could be re-used. She did not use traditional advertising but instead emphasised the company's stance against animal testing, supporting community trade and protecting the planet, long before global warming became a hotly debated issue.

As the company grew bigger Roddick used the platform to openly criticise what she considered the environmental insensitivity of the industry and traditional views of beauty. The company was sometimes considered anti-capitalist, but their philosophy aimed to promote international marketplaces, using its influence and profits for programmes such as Trade Not Aid.

The uncompromising campaigning activity led by Roddick, indirectly promoted The Body Shop which experienced rapid growth, expanding 50% annually. By 1991 the company's market value stood at £350 million, and it was largely credited with the banning of animal testing for cosmetic purposes in the UK. In March 2006, The Body Shop controversially agreed to a £652.3m takeover by L'Oreal with Roddick reputedly earning £130 million from the sale.

In September 2007, Dame Anita Roddick died aged 64. She donated her entire £51 million personal fortune to good causes before her death, with the remaining £665,747 consumed by inheritance tax, leaving her net worth as nil.

DON'T TRY THIS AT HOME

Marketing disasters – awareness

Cillit Bang

In October 2004, Cillit Bang (a household cleaner) was launched in the UK, after a successful trial in Hungary the previous year. Available in most major supermarkets, the packaging design was garish and simplistic and replicated the style of cheap packaging found in pound shops and discount outlets. JWT, the London advertising agency, was used to create a heavyweight television campaign using a cheesy, home shopping channel style, featuring Barry Scott. A high energy, over-enthusiastic presenter with a 'shouty' voice, he performed amazing demonstrations using the cleaner, most notably dipping a dirty penny in the product and seconds later revealing it, clean and shiny. The advert gave the impression that Barry fronted the company, and had come across an amazing formula that would revolutionalise household cleaning.

In the second series of ads JWT used the 'drama triangle' principle, where a person has a problem and a second party arrives to either solve that problem and 'rescue' them, or help them solve it for themselves. Barry is joined by stereotype housewife character Jill, who remarks of his penny-cleaning demonstration, "you love that one, Barry." In both editions of the commercial, Cillit Bang claims to remove limescale, rust and ground-in dirt in an instant.

Within a year of its launch, a quarter of all UK households (6 million) had bought the product[75]. In the first 18 months it had worldwide sales of £140 million[76]. But Cillit Bang and Barry Scott, weren't quite what the public thought they were. Whilst the ad gave the impression that Cillit Bang was a one-off product, it was in fact part of the huge stable of Reckitt Benckiser brands including Harpic, Airwick, Windolene, Dettol, Mr Sheen, Clearasil and Nurofen. Repeat purchases of the product had been at a very low 14%[77], with a number of complaints at its lack of effectiveness. Viewers complained that whilst the commercial claimed Cillit Bang could render a dirty coin as good as new in 15 seconds, this was misleading. The Advertising Standards Authority upheld the complaints.

With the popularity and cult following of Barry Scott, Reckitt Benckiser used the Cohn & Wolf public relations agency to ghost write a blog and post messages on other well known blogs. When it emerged that Barry Scott was a completely fictional character that had been invented by JWT, and that the messages had been left by members of the brand's PR team, bloggers were furious and the media was alerted. After two years, the lack of marketing authenticity began to seriously hit the brand and its sales.

---

[75] *Marketing*, 2 September 2006
[76] *Design Week*, 3 August 2006
[77] Europanel, April 2006

PART 6

WHERE CAN THEY FIND OUT MORE?

INFORMATION GATHERING EXPLAINED

Important note:
As previously stated the next three elements of the Isaiah Logic process – Information gathering, assessment and handover – have been separated out. However, it depends on your type of business and your organisational marketing needs, whether you go through each of these three in sequence and how much time elapses between each one. If you are a retail operation it is feasible that information gathering, assessment and handover happen in a matter of minutes, and they become 'fused' in the process. If however you are selling a service, capital goods, a message or a product that involves more than just pocket money, it is likely that your customer will go through each stage, sometimes with weeks or months elapsing before they make a purchase decision. No matter what your situation, it is still a good idea to understand each of these three elements, because even if they are 'fused' in the mind of your customer, you can still control their experience of each and better influence their decision making.

Fishing not hunting

The big advertising agencies that go for awareness to gain recognition of your service, product or message, will pretty much leave you on your own after the campaign has finished. They'll show you the statistics for customer recognition of your brand and you can track the sales figures or outcomes you set to see if it's worked. You should get an initial upturn in sales but will your new customers be convinced and go for a repeat purchase or recommend you to their friends through word of mouth? Even if you are 'selling' a social message or public sector service, will the campaign achieve lasting results? This is no concern of the advertising agency, they'll be on to the next client by then. But for you, this is just the start to gain *sustainable* outcomes or repeat purchases, not just the one off 'buy' out of curiosity. Most business people don't want simple brand awareness, they want customers, and they want them to return again and again.

If you have used an awareness campaign and over-claimed, when your customer goes on to use your product or service they will soon find out if you have been somewhat economical with the truth, or if you have plain misled them. The awareness campaign and the information you subsequently provide must be authentic. It has to be honest and fair and reflect the culture of your company and the nature of your operations, if it doesn't you will shoot yourself in the foot for the long term.

You have raised awareness of your name, so that a wide audience has your expertise and intellectual reputation stored in the back of their mind waiting to be aroused at a later date. To follow you need to sell the specific elements of your product, service or message in more detail. The aim from this point is to get the potential customer to draw on their previous subconscious impression, (*"I remember hearing about them from somewhere"*), and for them to want to find out more about the specific. Once achieved, your final aim is to get them to buy your product or service, step over your threshold in person or engage with your message. From this point the *Hand over* element takes over, see below.

The marketing of specifics is pretty neatly summed up by Dev and Schultz. They rightly believe that the outward push of promotional marketing is no longer relevant, and that getting particular product or service information across is:

"developing the means to give customers (or potential customers) the right information on the right subject at the right time on their terms." [78]

---

[78] Dev, Chekitan S. and Schulz, Don E., (Jan/Feb 2005) "Time to Kill Off the Four Ps?", *Marketing Management* magazine

Promotional 'push' marketing is usually unwanted on the part of the potential customer, it's pretty much discredited. You can guess that from the description – *push*. It's coming at us from all sides and it increasingly feels intrusive. You might get two people out of a hundred that are thrilled by the arrival of one of your direct mail leaflets, internet pop-up ads or home telesales call, because it's perfect timing and it's just what they've been looking for. But the downside is you've just annoyed 98 people who didn't want that leaflet/ad/phone call and now have to make the effort to get rid of it. That's 98 potential customers who are irritated by you, and they've been sacrificed for the sake of two.

I cannot understand a marketing manager that decides it's a legitimate and potentially successful strategy to thrust their product, or proposition, at me without my permission. It's just counter-productive. That's why the end bit of the above quotation is so important – *"on their terms"*. The other thing that strikes me is the pure waste. The title of this part of the Isaiah Logic is therefore intentional; it's not information provision by you, the marketer, it's the gathering of information by your potential customers or audience. They do the searching, and you must make sure it's there, in the format and language they want, when they go and look for it.

The following are the worst kind of marketing mediums that are the antithesis of customer information seeking and permission marketing:

- unsolicited direct mail, particularly inside magazines and newspapers
- unsolicited e-mails
- unsolicited faxes
- domestic telesales
- flyposting
- pop-up ads on the internet
- ads distributed via text message

If you advocate these mediums you could get a response rate as high as 5%, but it's more likely that it will be around 1% or less. If you think that's a good return, turn it on its head and look at it this way – you've just wasted 95% to 99% of your budget, not to mention 95% to 99% of your other resources including staff time.

The concept of "permission" was originally a term used in e-marketing, whereby marketers would set up a system to ask permission before they sent, or handed out, advertisements to prospective customers. The concept requires potential customers to 'opt-in' before you send them stuff, rather than forcing them to 'opt-out' only after they have received it. Permission marketing[79] was turned into a more rounded ideology by Seth Godin, the Purple Cow man. As part of this theory he also argued that the fragmentation of media had led to the loss of television as the dominant force. Is that really true?

Well, in 2006 Google took £900m in advertising revenue in the UK, compared with £800m at Channel 4. They earned £327m in the third quarter of 2007, compared to ITV's £317m and those figures are pre-credit crunch with mainstream media taking even more of a hit from collapsed marketing budgets. Globally Google is ten times bigger than General Motors (and not in as much trouble), more than three times bigger than McDonalds, 50% bigger than Coca-Cola, and worth $5 billion more than Procter & Gamble, the people who make Duracell batteries, Ariel washing powder, Crest toothpaste, Pringles potato chips, Olay skin care, Head and Shoulders, Wella hair care products, etc. So, yes it's obviously true and means that marketers no longer have the power to command the attention of anyone they choose, whenever they choose through a television screen. The chain created by churning out products, distributing them and consequently mass marketing them through television has irretrievably broken down. I strongly believe therefore, that in a marketplace where consumers have power and almost infinite choice, marketers must show more respect, i.e. no spam, no telesales, no deceit. You'll only annoy people.

Good marketing teams take time to work out what information the customer wants, in what style or language, how much of it, and what is the most convenient way to get at it. They know that

[79] Godin, S, (1999) *Permission Marketing*

customers want to access the details of the new product or service on their own terms, and the only place to find those clues is through the results of the insight research (see above). They might want to e-mail you and request a brochure, they might want to do their own research online, or they might want to talk it over with a real person. It really is detective work, looking for nuggets of useful insight, piecing things together and coming up with a multi-faceted, holistic programme of information provision.

For example, if I were interested in buying a new Mini car, how will I gain the information that will help me make my decision? As the manufacturer and the showroom dealer I have to make sure that I can respond to every request for information this potential customer may make over the coming weeks and months. Whether they are anonymously browsing online, personally requesting a brochure, are coming in to look around or want to speak to a salesperson. Potential customers will prefer to source information in different ways, and will gather the data over time before making such an important decision.

More emphasis must be given over to this part of the process, than is usual in marketing departments. This is the point where often a large part of the marketing budget is committed (and wasted), and although success can never be guaranteed, getting the thinking right will maximise your chances. It's fishing for customers. Choosing the right place, the right conditions, quietly and skilfully assembling the bait, allowing them to come to you when they're ready, giving them more and more until they're hooked. It's not 'running around with hob-nail-boots' type of advertising – hunting with a scatter gun, shooting anyone you come across in the hope that in the long run you might hit a target. The problem with that approach is when you eventually get a customer you never quite know why and you never learn anything, so you have to get your gun out and start again for the next campaign. Not a great recipe for an efficient use of financial resources in the long term[80].

---

[80] As an aside on this subject matter, marketers should be ashamed of themselves for the damage they do to the environment with all that pointless waste. I wouldn't be surprised, if the profession caused more global warming by the production of rarely seen bits of printed

If you used your insight work, looked at your advertising budget afresh and were corporately and socially responsible and ditched the unsolicited blanket use of direct mail, you never know you might get to use your brains instead and market in a planned and altogether more subtle way. It's also great customer service when every time they come back with another question, or another search for information it's right there for them when, where and how they want it.

Synopsis

Information gathering is providing the potential customer with honest information about a specific product or service in the right format, language and terms for them, so they can seek it out when they're ready.

Expert mining of the insight research and a true understanding of the customer, are the foundations of getting your product or service offering in front of them without being intrusive. Creating messages that capitalise on that knowledge, and choosing media channels to achieve stand out with subtlety and authority, from the white noise that competes for their attention, is a critical marketing skill. The conclusion of the information gathering stage, should allow the potential customer, to begin the process of assessment of your offer compared to others.

paper, than motorists.

HOW TO PROVIDE SUPERIOR INFORMATION

Where to get the best

At this point, you understand your customers, have refined your product or service and they're interest has been aroused by the awareness campaign you have conducted. The potential customer wants to find out more about your proposition – you've whetted their appetite but that's all so far. You need to provide them with honest information about a specific product or service in the right format, language and terms for them, so they can seek it out when they're ready.

In general this will mean brochures or product literature, web pages or maybe a customer information line. The key part to this element is to map how potential customers can interface with you; identify every single part of the organisation they come into contact with. Make sure everyone involved is trained and well-briefed, and that there is an efficient process for a response. If someone rings for a brochure, send it out within two working days. If they want to ask detailed technical questions make sure there is someone that can answer them. You have spent a lot of time, effort and money up until now, finally convincing a potential customer to contact your company. What's the point of all that effort, if no-one can be bothered to pick up the phone or reply to an e-mail enquiry?

Aside from one-to-one interaction, your passive marketing materials have to be beautifully designed. Use a professional, well-respected design agency that can produce wonderful design and can commission good photography and copywriting. You should also use them for print production and to oversee the printing process. Go through a tender process and (as discussed above for PR tendering), look for evidence that their previous design work has been effective and ask for references from their current clients. Everyone these days is highly design literate and can spot poor design and layout in an instant. They will assume that a shoddy brochure or leaflet equals shoddy product or service, so don't skimp by getting your daughter's design student boyfriend to do it.

If your customer base will be using the internet to research your offering, you need to pay this as much attention as if it was a printed brochure. Because the web is so transient and dynamic, organisations sometimes believe that it does not have to look as professional as their other company information, especially the written element. Nothing could be further from the truth. It is much harder to design because the user is in control of how they access and navigate the information you have provided. It is not linear like a page of printed text. Again it really is best to get in a professional web agency that can design the look and feel of your site (the front end), and ensure it is technically efficient and actually works (the back end). Discuss the key search words that you expect your customers to use, so that they can built into the back end design, and help you get higher up the search engine rankings. To choose agencies to tender for you, search out websites you really admire and find out who designed them.

Writing copy is not as easy as most people think. It's not about putting down your own thoughts, but writing in order to galvanise action by others, such as getting them to buy, convincing them to make a phone call, generally stimulating their interest and so on. Copy has to be as persuasive as possible to encourage the reader to start moving in the direction you want them to. As outlined in the Solution Development section of this book, your product or service solves a customer problem. Your copy must highlight the fact that you have sympathy for your potential buyer, empathising and explaining how this problem can be solved. You may also want to point out the challenges they will continue to face by not receiving your product or service. However, even if it's only one step in a complicated sales process, the copy is there for one reason only – to eventually get a sale.

On a budget

The bad news is you can't do this element on the cheap. You might be able to write your own copy and be proud of it, but make sure other people honestly think it is professional enough. Poor websites, badly written copy and so-so design will reveal your organisation in the worst possible light, so don't be tempted to cut corners, and don't use friends of friends. You need to get the professionals in, write a detailed brief of your requirements and tender for these services to get value for money. If budgets are tight, it's better to limit your ambitions than do it on the cheap: Have a website with just a few beautifully produced web pages. Don't print a 40 page brochure, produce a folder with single insert sheets that can be mixed and matched depending on customer requirements. Are you sure you need dozens of leaflets? Produce a couple of stunning ones instead.

Where to find design agencies

There will be a design agency somewhere in your area, so if you want the convenience of a local agency, make sure they produce good quality design by asking for references and following them up. The award winning ones can be found on the Design and Art Directors website at www.dandad.org/awards/ where there are dozens of categories including press, poster, print and magazine design. If you are using an individual designer, it's best to check that they are a member of the Chartered Society of Designers. You can perform a search at their site on www.csd.org.uk.

Design Week is regarded as the key industry magazine which has awards each year, which you can view at www.designweek.co.uk. The magazine has plenty of adverts and articles which showcase design agencies, as does *Creative Review*. Both magazines are available at national newsagents such as W.H. Smith.

Where to find web agencies

There are hundreds of small companies that will build a website for you, but you need to check that they have a good track record[81]. The more established ones, as mentioned above, can be found by visiting www.brandrepublic.com/revolution, which is the internet home page of *Revolution,* the web industry magazine. Online they have a supplier directory where you can search for agencies by discipline or location. You can buy *Webuser* magazine and use their recommendations to find sites that you like (visual appeal and usability), then research who designed and built them. Most agencies put their name at the bottom of the home page of the site they have designed. You can also find some of the best sites by visiting www.newstatesman.com, and looking at their past and present *New Media Award* winners.

Where to find copywriters

If you are using a design, PR, advertising or web agency, they will usually be able to supply, or recommend, a copywriter for you. This is the best course of action, as they're likely to be someone they've used for a long time, that they can trust and will be of a good standard. If not you could go onto the Institute of Copywriting website at www.inst.org and use their search facility.

Recommended further reading

- Ogilvy, D. (2007), *Ogilvy on Advertising*
- Maslen, A. (2007), *Write to Sell: The Ultimate Guide to Great Copywriting*
- For a step-by-step guide to improve sales conversion on your website – Eisenberg, B., Eisenberg, J., Davis, L. (2007), *Call to Action: Secret Formulas to Improve Online Results*

---

[81] If you ask a web designer or agency to buy a domain name for you (e.g. www.widget.com), insist that this is bought in your name, otherwise you won't officially own it, they will.

www.copyrighting.co.uk has some further information and debate on copywriting. If you can ignore the shameless self-promotion and dodgy photographs, it's worth taking a look at the free online e-guide that you can download.

OTHER THINGS TO CONSIDER

Environmental aspects of providing information

With increasing consumer awareness of climate change and environmental issues, companies should be adapting their marketing strategies to minimise their impact on the environment around them. You should believe this is the right thing to do anyway, but even if you're a bit of a Jeremy Clarkson and don't, it makes good business sense. Cars with big engines and high CO_2 emissions are astronomically expensive to run, now that fuel, car tax and punitive personal tax allowances have hit an all time high. Change your fleet cars, encourage paper, energy and water saving amongst your staff, and you will increase your profit margin immediately. You may also wish to consider:

- The environmental impact and cost of getting your product or service to your customer
- The use of fuel by your distribution company if this is outsourced, could they use a environmentally-friendly option than diesel
- Delivering in non-peak hours reducing time held up in traffic congestion.
- Minimising deliveries or journeys to customers, and using other forms of transport such as trains

If you truly believe in being environmentally responsible as an organisation, it's likely to have a positive impact on your image and reputation among customers. No more so, in the use of your marketing and packaging materials. Although you will take advice from designers, agencies and printers, you are the client and have control over the specification of your promotional or awareness campaigns. You should ensure that any tangible products or literature produced, reflect the environmental choice you have made. State on your stationery that it's made from recycled paper, make statements on e-mails that they shouldn't be printed out unless absolutely necessary, etc. In the area of packaging you will need to consider:

- The impact of production and the sourcing of materials
- Whether your suppliers use energy efficient and environmentally sound techniques
- Whether you are over-packaging some of your products
- Recyclable and/or bio-degradable materials

Some suggestions for environmentally preferable printing options include:

- **Recycled paper**. Ask your designer or printer to have your project printed on recycled papers, which will not compromise quality or cost. FSC certified papers are also an environmentally sound alternative to virgin paper.

- **Vegetable based inks**. Most printers will be able to print your work using vegetable based inks or low-alcohol inks as opposed to chemical based inks. These are kinder to the environment (as well as printing staff) and are easier to recycle.

- **Print finishing**. Laminated and UV-varnished products cannot always be recycled. Ask if there are any water-based coatings which will achieve the same effect.

- **Print sizes**. Does your project need to be a large size or can it be smaller, or does it have to have that many pages? A reduced format will save paper, ink, water and carbon emissions when distributed, and will also save money on production costs and postage. If you are keen to have a non-standard size, try a format that won't have too much trimming and waste.

- **Shelf life.** Try to produce marketing materials that will have a reasonably long shelf life, or can be updated easily. So much stationery and so many brochures and leaflets are ordered in huge quantities because it appears to work out cheaper per unit. This is a false economy. Only order what you will use, and look at a design and binding method that allows you to update regularly without a full reprint.

You should also examine whether you are making an environmental impact on the immediate community, as this will most certainly affect your reputation. If your company makes excessive noise or smells can these be minimised? Is your site a monumental eyesore that could be camouflaged or tidied up?

Corporate social responsibility

Corporate social responsibility (CSR) or corporate citizenship, encourages organisations to consider the interests of society by taking responsibility for the impact of their actions on customers, suppliers, employees, stakeholders and communities, as well as more generally on the environment. This is seen as not being driven by legislation, but more as a voluntary stance to improve the quality of life for individuals and communities. There are legal duties on employers in relation to environmental protection, health and safety and employment rights, but CSR goes beyond these basic obligations[82]. It could be a useful tactic to outline your approach to CSR and to demonstrate it clearly in the provision of company information.

There have been many studies and much debate on the topic. Supporters believe that ultimately it leads to better business performance in the long term, winning customers and reducing risk. They believe that CSR is an investment in a strategic direction or a distinctive capability which can be measured by increased reputation and decreased risk. Some seek to agree a financial model

---

[82] Visit the government's CSR website at www.csr.gov.uk. There is also useful information on www.forumforthefuture.org.uk and www.accountability.org.uk.

to value these intangible assets on a balance sheet. Critics say that it is not the principle role of a business to do this, but instead to create purely economic benefits. As one Russian businessman put it:

"The purpose of a company is to earn shareholder return. It is not to improve the lot of the people . . . I would like to question the utility of corporate social responsibility beyond marketing and the CEO wanting to be well received at the golf club."[83]

Personally I believe that companies, and in particular very large companies, have a genuine responsibility to minimise their environmental impact where it is practically and financially feasible, and think carefully how they treat their suppliers, customers and employees. There is an obvious ethical argument here, but also one of risk minimisation and the protection of reputation and therefore shareholder value. Surely the dismal state of the economy is in large part due to unethical trading practices or financially irresponsible machismo which belied the caring, sharing, trusting, literature and advertising.

One of the main themes of Isaiah Logic is if you aren't authentic with your marketing messages it will backfire at some point in the future. We are seeing that in the most spectacular fashion right now. If within the law, organisations want to trash the environment, treat their employees badly and sell duff products they are perfectly entitled to do so, but if they present a marketing façade that is very different, they will most definitely be found out in the long run.

Even if you are not personally persuaded by the ethical and environmental arguments, many consumers are, and it is increasingly being seen as a smart strategy to win more sales. Naturally, as more and more buyers are choosing to use companies with genuine CSR credentials, those that are adopting them late have been accused of cynical marketing tactics.

.

---

[83] Stefano Vlahovic, of the Russian pre-packaged food business Produkty Pitania, at a public panel discussion at the European Bank for Reconstruction and Development Annual Meeting in 2004.

THAT'S THE WAY TO DO IT

Real life information gathering examples

BMW's Mini

The original Mini was first produced by the British Motor Corporation in 1959, designed by Sir Alec Issigonis. The original is considered a symbol of the 1960s, and its innovative space-saving front-wheel-drive layout, allowed 80% of the area of the car's floorplan to be used for passengers and luggage thus allowing more room in a smaller space. Sales were slow to start but by the mid-sixties the Mini proved something of an icon, with film and pop stars popularising the car as a fashion item.

This was firmly sealed when the Mini Cooper S won the Monte Carlo Rally in 1964, 1965 and 1967 and when it was arguably the star of the 1969 film *The Italian Job*, (it featured prominently in an elaborate car chase in which a gang of thieves drive three Minis down staircases, through storm drains, over buildings and finally into the back of a moving bus).

It soon became the most popular British car ever, but it never made money for its makers because it sold at less than its production cost. This may have been necessary in order to compete with its rivals, but it is rumoured that it was due to an accounting error.

By the late 1970s the Mini began to look outdated in the face of newer and more practical rivals including the VW Polo and the Renault 5. Reports of the Mini's imminent demise surfaced in 1980 with the launch of the Austin Metro. Although the Mini continued after the Metro's launch, production volumes were reduced as British Leyland and its successor Austin Rover concentrated on the Metro as its key supermini.

In 1994 BMW took control of Rover but suffered massive losses leading it to break up the group in March 2000, selling

Landrover to Ford, and Rover to a British consortium for £10. However, BMW retained the Mini name and continued with its plans for a new model. The last 'old' Mini was built that year with a total of 5,387,862 Mini cars having been manufactured.

BMW didn't keep the Mini because it had innovative engineering or solid build quality, they kept it for its inherent differentiation and great marketing potential; a huge asset which allows for premium pricing and hence the budget to pay for design, innovation and marketing. They carefully highlighted its British heritage (you can even order one with a Union Jack on the roof), and decided to allow for maximum buyer customisation.

This was an extremely important marketing tactic, as whilst this was to be a commodity car – selling in its millions, its desirability needed to ironically hinge on its individuality, thereby reducing the feeling that lots of people own one. In order to facilitate this, BMW Group introduced an online ordering system for dealerships, with customers being able to view their customisations on screen, (you can also do this on their website), changing its colour, wheels, etc. and getting an immediate price. There are more than ten million possible variations, and every element is explained in detail for those considering a purchase, or indulging in a bit of screen envy (window shopping).

At the dealership they can then confirm the delivery date on the spot, and within in a few seconds your place in the production process is immediately reserved. BMW has optimised internal processes so that changes (upholstery, sound system, engine capacity, etc.) can be accommodated up to ten days before the production begins without affecting the delivery date.

On 3rd April 2007, the one millionth new Mini rolled out of the Oxford Plant after six years of production.

THAT'S THE WAY TO DO IT

Real life information gathering examples

MyTravel

MyTravel is one of the UK's leading holiday and leisure groups with brands including Airtours, Going Places and Mytravel.com. In 2005 they decided to go through a significant reworking of their website. The three stage re-design began with a launch of the first phase in December 2005. The work involved extensive user testing. Reviewers examined MyTravel websites and also the sites of its competitors, establishing the most important aspects of website design for the travel industry.

Users wanted richer content with relevant images, 360-degree virtual tours of resorts and accommodation, video footage, maps, weather, and greater detailed information on activities and facilities. MyTravel also wanted to make the online booking activity easier to navigate and cut down the actual booking time, with the number of steps needed to make a reservation reduced from eight to five.

The project resulted in reduced booking times by up to 40% and a 20% improvement in buying conversion levels across all MyTravel's websites[84].

---

[84] Usabilitynews.com, 11 August 2006

DON'T TRY THIS AT HOME

Marketing disasters – information gathering

Standard Life

Standard Life's Pension Sterling Fund was a godsend for beleaguered savers, desperately looking for a safe haven in a low risk cash fund towards the end of 2008. The glossy literature described the fund as wholly invested in cash, and to some it was an ideal way of moving their pension savings into a fund on a short term basis, before buying an annuity for their retirement. A drop in value would mean a lower pension income. As it turned out, it was actually invested in asset-backed securities and the £2.4 billion fund lost 4.8% in a single day.

After many complaints and some negative press, the company admitted that the literature supporting the fund "fell short of our own high standards".[85] Standard Life at first refused to consider compensation, even though their publicity materials were clearly misleading. However, in February 2009, it announced a change of heart and boosted the fund value by £100 million, to restore customers' losses.

---

[85] *Which Magazine*, April 2009

PART 7

HOW DO YOU COMPARE TO THE COMPETITION?

ASSESSMENT EXPLAINED

Baaaa is humbug

Even during financially hard times, generally the UK population is relatively better off than ever. There's also an increasing awareness that as people become more affluent, they don't want to keep up with the Jones's like they used to. In fact the opposite is happening. They want to assert their individuality, not celebrate their sameness. If the guy next door roars home in a Porsche Boxster, even if you were just about to buy one yourself, you would go out of your way to choose something different. If money equals neighbourhood status, you exert that power by showing how individual you can afford to be, not how much of a sheep you are. Baaaa.

The launch of the new Mini, which BMW were careful to retain when they sold Rover for a tenner, is a good example of capitalising on the desire for consumer individuality. BMW knew that if designed and marketed well, the Mini would be a huge success. But if there were too many of them, and they all looked the same, it would soon lose its cachet and desirability and become a commodity car, like a Ford Focus. They went for individualisation in a big way. You can choose 18 different roof graphics for your new mini from a Union Jack, to tiger or zebra stripes, zips or tartan. There are bonnet graphics, different combinations of lights, spoilers, wheels, gear knobs, mats, dashboards and so on. There are hundreds of variations which lead to almost countless ways to achieve an individual car. So while they have sold over a million Minis, it doesn't feel like a commodity.

The self-empowering impact of the internet and the response of savvy organisations to individualisation, means people are increasingly expecting products and services to reflect their own personal tastes and preferences. You can even get 46,000 variations of coffee in Starbucks. Organisations need to look at a greater degree of flexibility in their product or service offerings to achieve success. Customers need to feel that there is an amount of tailoring around their own needs, but most importantly are being treated as an individual, not like sheep.

If you're promoting a new commodity product like biscuits, the customer is likely to fork out 70p, because they've heard of it and it's new, and kick into touch whatever they bought last week just to give it a try. Marketing in the fast moving consumer goods (fmcg) arena[86] is generally therefore hyper-competitive with little real differentiation between products. In this respect the public are notoriously promiscuous and change partners often. This type of marketing is big on awareness and "bringing the horse to water". It's about shouting very loud indeed, often using the muscle of a multi-million pound budget (television, radio, magazine advertising), and if someone has remembered the name and recognise the packet, Bob's your uncle. In the context of their £120 weekly shop, they might just give it a go, because they don't feel they have anything much to lose.

If the product is crap, they won't ever buy it again, but in this scenario that's not the responsibility of the advertising agency hired by the manufacturer, so they don't have to worry about that. In fmcg you needn't trouble yourself about customer service either, because some other poor bugger has to do that, and it doesn't have to impinge on your thought process or budget. Leave that to Asda, W.H. Smith or Boots the Chemist.

However, once people have to part with a few thousand pounds or even a twenty pound note, or have to buy a huge machine for a new factory or decide to follow some advice on public health, gathering information becomes critical. The irony is, packet soups, sandwich spreads, lipstick and fizzy drinks (fmcg), are the glory end of marketing and get the most budget and the most text books written about them. That's the bit of marketing you go into when you've been to Oxbridge. But it's relatively easier than other forms

---

[86] Fast Moving Consumer Goods, those everyday products that are cheap and sell quickly, usually in a retail setting, such as cosmetics or pre-packaged food.

of marketing, because often it's more about the awareness stage, than information gathering, assessment or customer service. It's not that fmcg is less important, it's just that you only need some of the marketing skills not the whole set. Service and business-to-business marketing, and most especially public social campaigns, require a more sophisticated, end-to-end engagement of the audience that doesn't stop short at awareness. Depressingly, all too many non-fmcg organisations stop at the awareness part too, reckoning that at that juncture it's "job done" as far as their definition of marketing is concerned.

Fast-moving means the product doesn't stay with us for very long, it's been eaten or used by the next week or fortnight, by which time we need another fix. Things that cost more are around more. If we make a mistake, it'll be there looking at us for ages, with our spouse constantly reminding us we've been duped. In higher education, if a student makes the wrong purchasing decision (a full time degree is going to cost about £30k all told), it has the potential to be a serious set-back that could affect personal relationships and their professional future. It's therefore a very, very important purchasing decision. If I'm going to spend a fortune on a wedding, or taking my family out for a meal, I want it to be perfect in every way – the food, the service, the ambience and so on. If I've been sent abroad for a new machine for our factory it's the same. I will feel responsible if I've made the wrong choice. I will feel I've let everyone else down. It's not really about the money with 'experience' purchases, and I can't repeat that day again. "Wham, bam, thank you ma'am" fmcg marketing doesn't apply here.

There are two sorts of purchases – tangible and intangible. You see what you get with a tangible purchase, you part with your money and you instantly own, or receive, the thing you paid for; a car, a newspaper, a bottle of bleach, a machine, pair of shoes or a bag of chips. But you don't when it's intangible, you make a commitment by handing over the cash, but you don't know for sure what you're going to get. If I buy a holiday or a day's parachuting experience, I don't really know what it's going to be like, so I need lots of reassurance. I need it to be made tangible for me. I want photographs, testimonials, reviews, information on the climate, value for money, facilities and so on for me to make a decision. When I've made a commitment I also want some tangibility to assure me I've made the right choice – send me a confirmation letter or congratulate me on my choice by e-mail.

If you've completed the awareness activity, your name should be known at least sub-consciously, and information gathering should make it easy for potential customers to get more detail of the specific things they're interested in. When they've accessed or received that stuff, the assessment process has started. But what you really want as an outcome of the initial assessment, is for your customer to make a purchase remotely, or for them to engage with you, or come and visit you.

Let's say a customer is buying your make of car: During the showroom visit they will try and work out why it's different and distinct from the other cars they've researched. As part of that process they will also be taking in your sales techniques and other influencing factors, such as the showroom environment, how the salesperson is dressed and tone of voice they use, how long you made them wait or the quality of the publicity materials. They will test and weigh up your claims of differentiation or tangible benefits. They're literally 'shopping' at this point and shopping is about discrimination by comparison. The same happens for an intangible product or service, such as a walk-in health centre or a holiday when you go to see a travel agent, or you pop in to a restaurant to make your first reservation there.

For some services or products this shopping expedition is generally where most of the assessment takes place, and for your organisation it's where the 'sale conversion' process happens. It's where your customer measures those qualities that determine worth, usefulness, desirability and suitability. You have to make sure that you stand up well to the comparative factors that they (not you) prioritise in their assessment process. The assessment may not involve price, it may be about personal benefits, the time saving nature of the product or service, or the overall experience. After the expense and time-consuming effort of awareness raising and providing information, you've managed to get them there, now the real work starts in converting 'the sale'.

Synopsis

Assessment is where the potential customer works out the value of the product or service proposition put to them. The peripheral offerings (the add-ons, the sales person, the surroundings, etc.) and comparison with the competition are key factors in the assessment decision.

Potential customers work out the value of a product or service based on a variety of factors, which are not always just about price. They look to assess their worth, usefulness, desirability, suitability and importance. They want to compare and differentiate it from similar offerings and work out the total sacrifice they will need to make in order to acquire it. In the process they want reassurance they're making the right choice, and depending on the product or service, could be looking for an opportunity for individualisation, or at least the recognition that they are an individual.

HOW TO INFLUENCE ASSESSMENT

Where to get the best

This element may not apply to your type of business, but if it does, this is where the buying decision is finally made. The good news with this part of Isaiah Logic is that you don't need a huge budget, just dogged determination to insist it is done. It also includes your selling techniques. Are your sales people really well trained? Have they the right personality? If you want to re-evaluate your sales operation, you can ask a consultancy to train your sales people to achieve better results. This isn't about hard selling, just making sure you get sustainable results through superior customer relationship management.

On a budget

Potential customers have been persuaded by your awareness campaign, and wowed by your website or the literature you sent. They are assessing your proposition against the competition, and in many cases will come and visit your premises. If you have a showroom, a reception area or offices, what do they really look like? What is the full sensory experience they will receive, including what they see, hear, taste, touch and smell?

When they arrive, is it easy to find where they need to go? Is your signage broken or dirty, or the parking area litter-strewn or the entrance to your reception clogged up with the sound and smell of your staff smoking, chatting and laughing? Are your cups chipped or does your coffee taste awful? Are there loo rolls and soap in the toilets? Are the brochures you have laid out, in pristine condition? Every part of this experience is helping your customer to decide whether to do business with you. It is as much a part of your brand and your corporate identity as your stationery, livery or signage.

Before they arrived they may have been 95% certain of making a purchase, but have you put them off at the last hurdle?

It's easy to have a one-off blitz and insist that these areas are up to scratch in a high level purge, probably involving a lick of paint. The trick is to make sure they stay that way, every day, every week, every year. Implement a system that can be checked and assessed easily, make someone responsible and ensure it is known that it's a high priority. It's not easy to see something anew if you've been walking through the same set of doors for years. But try to look at these areas with fresh eyes as often as you can. Try to be a customer.

In relation to your product or service, are you sure that the add-ons or the customisations available, have been explained openly and honestly? Many customers feel cheated when they add up the true cost of acquiring your offering, and find it to be much more expensive than they realised.

Where to find an interior designer

Obviously if you are going to give your reception area and car park a good clean up and lick of paint, you will not need an interior designer, but if you feel a complete refurbishment is in order, or that you need advice on furniture, floor coverings and other design elements to promote the visitor experience you will need a professional, who will look at it from a customer perspective. The British Interior Design Association has a website at www.bida.org and has a search facility where you can find a designer by specialism and location.

Where to find sales training consultancies

There are hundreds of organisations that deliver sales training. One of the best ways to make sure you find a good one, is by word of mouth recommendation. If you do not know anyone who could give you a referral, go to the local Chamber of Commerce to ask if they have members who deliver sales training, but ask for references and follow them up. If you want to send members of staff to sales seminars to stimulate their thinking and give them a good grounding in sales techniques, it may be worth joining the Institute of Sales and Marketing Management (ISMM). Once your organisation is a member, your staff can attend their seminars for free.

Recommended further reading

The Business Balls website has a comprehensive section on sales and selling at www.businessballs.com/salestraining.htm. Not only does it have a sales training specification template, it more or less goes through every technique you would ever need. The two books below are easy to read and will help you achieve better results almost immediately.

- Southon, M., West, C. (2005), *Sales on a Beermat*
- Morgen, S.D., (1999), *Selling with Integrity: Reinventing Sales Through Collaboration, Respect and Serving*

OTHER THINGS TO CONSIDER

The buying decision making process

To understand how your customers make an assessment of your product, service or your organisation as a whole, helps you manipulate the buying decision making process.

Isaiah Logic is an attempt at a new marketing process, one that helps business people, but from the perspective of the customer, which in most cases means the buyer. The inspiration and perspective has come from consumer buying behaviour and the generation of positive word of mouth recommendation, which it logically should. Yet whilst many books and studies attempt to explain why we prefer one brand over another or buy what we do, in reality it's almost impossible to predict how the public react. Let's face it, would you have put your mortgage on developing Beanie Babies, the Rubik cube or Riverdance?

There is an often-quoted buying decision making process shown below, which is popular with marketers and is largely based on the EKB Model[87]. It divides our decision to buy a product or service into five stages and has been influential in developing the Isaiah Logic process:

Problem recognition

Perceiving a need, which is usually the difference between a person's ideal situation and their actual situation. It can be as simple as noticing that you're running out of milk or it can be activated by marketing efforts.

---

[87] The Engel-Kollat-Blackwell Model – Engel, J., Kollat, D., Blackwell, R. (1978), *Consumer Behaviour*. Updated – Engel, J., Blackwell, R., Miniard, P. (2000), *Consumer Behaviour*.

Information search

This clarifies the options open to the consumer. If they have experience of a product or service that may be adequate to decide on the action to take. If not an external search is required because past knowledge or experience is not sufficient. This can include personal information sources from friends and family which amount to word of mouth recommendation. Public sources, such as online rating sites, consumer reports or guides like *Which?* Magazine and *The Good Beer Guide*, and marketing sources such as advertising and websites.

Evaluation of alternatives

When the information search has been conducted the alternatives need to be evaluated. The search clarifies the problem for the potential buyer by suggesting criteria to use for the purchase, possibly yielding brand names that might meet those criteria. Their perception of value is influenced by objective attributes (such as price) against subjective values (such as prestige).

The information search and evaluation of alternatives will depend on the level of involvement of the consumer and the personal, social and economic significance of the purchase. A high involvement purchase will typically be very expensive, have serious personal consequences or could reflect on the buyer's social image.

Purchase decision

The purchase decision is evolving and now there are three alternatives; who to buy from, when to buy or not to buy at all. The eventual decision is based on a number of situational factors including social pressure (if others are with you to make the purchase) or physical surroundings such as décor or crowding. There are also believed to be temporal effects such as the time of day or the amount of time available, and antecedent states (the consumers mood and whether they have cash on hand, etc.)

Post-purchase behaviour

After buying a product, the consumer compares it with expectations and is either satisfied or dissatisfied. This will obviously affect perceptions of value, their communication of that value to others and their repeat purchase behaviour. Some companies work to produce positive post-purchase communications to try to convince buyers that they made the right decision.

Maslow's Hierarchy of Needs

As with the buying decision making process, models of consumer behaviour can help contextualise the solution development activity. The classic model is Maslow's famous Hierarchy of Needs[88] (see below), a broad interpretation of basic human needs expressed in five clear stages[89].

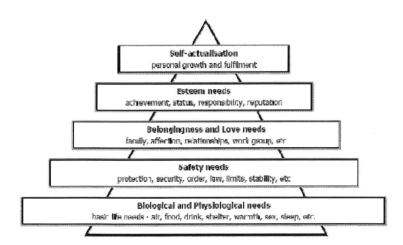

---

[88] Maslow, A. (1954), *Motivation and Personality*
[89] There are seven and eight level Hierarchy of Needs models, which are later adaptations by others. Arguably though, the original five-level model includes the later additional sixth, seventh and eighth ('Cognitive', 'Aesthetic', and 'Transcendence') levels within the original 'Self-Actualization' level 5.

Maslow observed that these needs must be satisfied in the given order. If for example Biological and Physiological needs (level 1) are satisfied, we aim and drive towards the next level need. Further he believed that the thwarting of needs is usually a cause of stress, and is particularly so at level 4. Using a work example, this theory postulates that you can't easily motivate someone to work as a team member (level 3) when their house is being re-possessed (level 1). The implication for marketing is that if you recognise these basic needs, messages can be adapted to prompt buyer behaviour, or help an organisation establish the importance of their product or service on the scale. Hence:

Physiological needs

Food, drink, heating, housing, sex and sleeping aids, beds and bedding.

Safety needs

Security products and services, legal services, insurance products inc. life and home.

Belongingness and Love needs

Dating services, chat-lines, clubs, teams, religion, societies, memberships.

Esteem needs

Cosmetics, fast cars, lifestyle products and services, fashion.

Self-Actualisation needs

Self improvement and education

There are a number of other models which are not as broad, and more tightly focused on brand preference and consumer behaviour including the Howard-Sheth model[90].

---

[90] Sheth, J.N., Howard, J.A., (1969), The Theory of Buyer Behaviour. See also The Sheth Model

Sales and marketing and the law

Obviously as a business you will need to ensure you conform to the laws of copyright and contract, or anything that specifically relates to your industry (such as the control of gambling or money-lending). In addition, you should be familiar with the Data Protection Act 1998[91] and, particularly if you are in the public sector, the Freedom of Information Act 2000[92]. If you are packaging your own goods, or are in the food sector selling loose products you will need to conform to the incoherent Weights and Measures Legislation[93], which is currently being reformed.

As an organisation providing goods or services, you also need a basic understanding of *The Consumer Protection Act 1987*[94] and the *Supply of Goods and Services Act 1982*[95], especially in relation to product liability and consumer safety. *The Trade Descriptions Act 1968*[96], *Control of Misleading Advertisements Regulations 1988*[97] and large parts of the *Consumer Protection Act* are designed to protect buyers from misleading adverts and unfair selling techniques. If all these regulations are too much for you, then a good rule of thumb is not to lie or overclaim, and make sure that any products or services that you provide are as safe as possible. If something does go wrong however, claiming a lack of awareness of the law is no defence.

Basically, the *Trades Description Act* declares that any description of goods that you sell or hire, or services that you provide, must be accurate. That description could be in writing (for example in an advertisement), in an illustration (for example on packaging), or given verbally (for example in a sales pitch). The description itself covers a range of factors including:

---

of Family Decision-Making – Sheth, J.N., (1974), Models of Buyer Behaviour

[91] For more information go to the Information Commissioner's Office at www.ico.gov.uk

[92] Visit www.foi.gov.uk for more details

[93] Visit the website of the National Weights and Measures Laboratory for further information at www.nwml.gov.uk/Legislation.aspx

[94] See www.berr.gov.uk – the Department for Business, Enterprise and Regulatory Reform.

[95] Ibid

[96] Ibid

[97] See www.oft.gov.uk – the Office of Fair Trading

- quantity and size
- composition
- method, place and date of manufacture
- fitness for stated purpose
- endorsements by people or organisations

In May 2008, the *Consumer Protection from Unfair Trading Regulations* came into force, effectively replacing many areas of the previous legislation. The main enforcement body is the Office of Fair Trading, who use Trading Standards officers to seek out non-compliance, however under certain circumstances the Financial Services Authority and the Consumers' Association have statutory powers and could enforce the law. Penalties can be imposed on companies or senior individuals up to £5,000 who "consented or connived" in the offence, and imprisonment is possible.

If a selling or marketing practice was believed to be illegal, (even if a company were not prosecuted), insurers may disclaim liability for any related losses, or a supplier may claim a contract null and void. Whichever way you look at it, it's best to understand the potential ramifications of the legislation and ensure compliance. Given some of the case studies in this book, you should by now be persuaded to only use marketing tactics that are authentic and ethical. If you don't you will be caught out at some point, it's just a matter of when. If buyer trust is dented, your reputation will suffer and so will your sales.

Below are some highlights of the new legislation which need investigating in detail, if you wish to use these tactics for your next marketing campaign.

- The new laws give specific protection for 'vulnerable' consumers such as the disabled, children and the elderly. You now need to take into consideration whether your advertising may affect them unfairly, for example if you have small print that someone with poor eyesight may not be able to read.
- Any marketing or advertising activity that directly influences children to buy your products, or to persuade their parents or other adults to buy them, is a new criminal offence.

Sometimes described as 'pester power', it does not mean that advertising to children is outlawed, but the use of lines such as 'Ask Dad to buy XYZ' is not allowed.

- It is now illegal to falsely claim that a product or service is only available for a limited period. If your stocks are likely to remain fairly constant, you cannot state "buy now, while stocks last".
- Offering a prize in a promotion without actually awarding it, could be liable to prosecution.
- Product placement has some new regulatory additions, especially regarding made-for-internet programmes. It will become unlawful unless transparently obvious or stated up front that it is a placement.

Your staff cannot pose as a consumer. Recent viral marketing tactics, such as using staff to blog or highlight deals, will effectively become illegal. They now need to disclose their commercial interest.

THAT'S THE WAY TO DO IT

Real life assessment examples

eBay

The online auction web site was originally named AuctionWeb and was founded in San Jose, California in 1995 by Pierre Omidyar in his spare bedroom. The very first item sold was a broken laser pointer for $14.83. Omidyar had a consulting company called Echo Bay and tried to register the domain name, but it was already taken so he shortened it to eBay, registering it in 1997. The website offers several type of auctions where the seller offers one of more items for sale for a specified number of days, with the seller being able to establish a reserve price. The fixed price 'auction' allows buyers to purchase items at a set fee.

eBay has established detailed rules about bidding, retraction of bids, shill bidding (collusion to drive up the price), and other aspects which it claims to monitor carefully. In reality it is the eBay community of users that 'police' the site. Sellers are rated by those who buy their good, using a star system from 1 to 5, with 5 being very good. Buyers can also leave comments on the service they received and the condition of the received item.

There are nearly 8m users in the UK, with 100m worldwide. At any given time there are about 2m items listed on www.ebay.co.uk. Amongst the more unusual items listed have been a 50,000 year old mammoth (sold for £61,000), a Dr Who tardis, an individual chicken nugget that was supposed to be 'lucky', Britney Spears used bubble gum and a whole town in America. A man offered one of his kidneys for auction, and another his wife. The most expensive item sold on the UK website was Lady Thatcher's handbag (£103,000), and globally a Gulfstream Jet (£3.2m).

eBay generates revenue through its fee system, earning commission on each sale, plus the fees it charges for everything from listing items to setting a reserve price. It handles trade worth $34b a year in 32 international markets and its 135m registered members buy or sell goods worth $1,050 every second, from over 34m items listed at any time. Omidayar hasn't run the company for some time, but remains as its Chairman. Forbes magazine values his personal worth at $10b.

eBay is a classic example of a platform that allows potential customers to compare and contrast products for sale. Allowing them to calculate worth, usefulness, desirability, suitability and importance. Photographs, layout, page design, testimonials and individualised text are intangible methods to elicit trust in the seller and the quality of their product.

THAT'S THE WAY TO DO IT

Real life assessment examples

HMV Group

A significant number of people have been buying (or stealing) their music, films and games over the internet – downloading their favourite stuff to play on MP3 players and computers. With the music industry slow to respond, the retailers have been put in a hugely difficult position. High street sales of pre-recorded music have fallen by 14% between 2002 and 2007[98]. The market shrank for the third consecutive year in 2007, dropping by 2.9% to £4 billion. At the same time downloads are rocketing, with predictions that sales will reach £600 million in value by 2012, accounting for 13.5% of the total music and video market in the UK[99]. Virgin pulled out of its megastore business because of the pressures. It was acquired by Zavvi Entertainment Group, which alongside Music Zone and Fopp soon called in the administrators.

HMV has been a leading music retailer since it opened its original Oxford Street store in 1921. Eighty or so years later it has 250 stores in the UK and a further 129 outlets internationally. After a major review of its brand, HMV decided to reinvent its stores as social hang outs and physical gateways to access catalogues of music, video and software games. Under Chief Executive Simon Fox, a strategic plan for the group involved a heavy commitment to retail design investment, with a key element of the plans to 'revitalise' its stores business, chiefly by embracing the consumer shift to digital products and online social networking.

To test the concept, a trial store opened in Dudley in the

---

[98] Mintel
[99] Verdict Research

West Midlands in September 2007. Technology played a substantial part, with social hubs connecting customers to the internet via Apple iMacs and digital kiosks enabling customers to purchase MP3 format songs as well as the ability to download video and games clips for free. The aim was to create a social space rather than the traditional concept of a shop.

THAT'S THE WAY TO DO IT

Real life assessment examples

Oskar

Within a year of its launch in 2000, Oskar was the third largest mobile phone operator in the Czech Republic, but they wanted to increase retail transactions to attract more young consumers in a mobile phone market, fast-approaching saturation point. They decided to structure their shops as homes with a very open plan feel. They removed all service counters and instead installed all-in-one pods to combine cash desks with interactive self-help tools designed to break down barriers between staff and customers.

A 'self-expression area' was also introduced in every store allowing customers to write messages on a wall. Store windows offered unobstructed views into the store over low-level plasma screens playing the latest campaigns and promotions. There was a significant investment in staff training to ensure their behaviour reinforced the new retail experience. Three pilot stores were opened soon after. Due to its resounding success, a national roll-out followed.

The new design attracted significantly more spontaneous visits, and customers browsed in-store for longer. Sales in redesigned stores rose by 10%, and 98% of visitors felt positive about the retail environment compared with 81% before the re-design. Meanwhile, nine out of ten visitors said they could more easily find what they were looking for – an increase of 27%.

In June 2005, at pre-credit crunch price levels, Oskar was acquired by Vodafone.[100]

DON'T TRY THIS AT HOME

Marketing disasters – assessment

Opulence Bar

The launch of an up market cocktail and champagne bar appealing to wealthy twenty-somethings in a rich suburb of Manchester requires some slick pre-opening PR and a grand opening night party. Opulence Bar had undergone an impressive re-fit, and promised nights of luxury with "soulful funky house, live bands and exquisite cocktails all decorated with sublime surroundings". Three house 'mixologists' had been employed to mix cocktails, and there was a private upstairs VIP bar. The opening night, restricted to key journalists and VIPs was set to be impressive, Opulence claimed it would be the "most extravagant opening ever". How would the journalists and VIPs assess it?

Altrincham is around ten miles from the middle of Manchester, but the tram runs from the city centre to the station – just five minutes walk from the new bar. Opulence chartered a tram to transport journalists and VIP guests from Manchester Piccadilly to Altrincham. According to British Trams Online, this was "the first time a tram had been

---

[100] A case study published by The Brand Union, as found on www.thebrandunion.com

specifically chartered for a private party". The PR blurb stated that the event would be sponsored by Krug and: "We're planning to roll out the red carpet, temporarily upholster the seats, and provide onboard entertainment for guests."

The grand opening event for VIPs arrived. These people are busy and they had all 'bought' the advertising and their expectations of the experience had been created. This is the press report from the highly influential Manchester Confidential, which was pretty much echoed by all the others:

"It sounded promising with a special tram – 'the Opulence Express' – laid on to swoosh city centre folk to the event: shame that the 'Express' resembled a BR Sprinter train from the eighties with a few Carpet World off-cuts on the floor. It got worse when the tram overshot the red carpet laid out at Altrincham station by twenty metres. Fortunately a pair of giggling hoodies picked it up and instead of nicking it, lugged it down to the correct location. Just when (you) didn't think anything else could go wrong, it did. The whole guest list was locked out of the bar for half an hour as finishing touches were applied. Most people buggered off to the adjacent Slug and Lettuce for a drink."

The Opulence Bar pre-publicity for the opening event, ridiculously over-claimed and under-delivered. To make an impact in the luxury market everything has to be right to justify the premium pricing, and woo clients with the kind of money and jobs most of us lust after. Unfortunately, the opening wasn't the only disaster, their glossy advert in a local upmarket magazine stated "the only bar outside of London to offer Kristal and Kruge Champagne by the glass." Our well-educated and moneyed potential clientele know that it's actually Cristal and Krug. Opulence Bar closed six months after opening and someone must have lost a fortune.

PART 8

WHAT ARE YOU LIKE TO DEAL WITH?

HANDOVER EXPLAINED

Do what it says on the tin

This part of the Isaiah Logic process is rarely talked about in the same breath as sales and marketing, and yet it's the real moment of truth. In comparison to other elements, practically no budget is ever dedicated to it in most organisations, and yet it's often the thing which customers remember the most. Word of mouth will always be the best marketing tool, so if you want to develop a great reputation, the point of handover is very important; not an afterthought in the marketing process but the culmination of all that effort. I also believe that if handover is good, it can contribute to how the customer subsequently views the value of their purchase or the consequent experience. Put simply, if a customer is dealt with efficiently and effectively at the point of sale, or in the first couple of weeks if it's a service, they will give you the benefit of the doubt for quite some time if other elements subsequently fail them. This part is where the sale really takes place, and so it has to be part of the marketing process, because its impact on true engagement or repeat purchases and word of mouth marketing is inestimable.

The hand over is where the product or service is *handed over* to the customer. OK they've already bought it, or decided to buy it, but now they take possession. You must do *exactly* what you said you would and it must be exactly what you said it would be. In some cases it's not a single transaction; that is to say a one-to-one experience when the customer pays for the goods and instantly receives them. In many service businesses hand over is the point when a potential customer has made their assessment, and has mostly decided to buy whatever it is you offer, but they can still back out at the last minute. From that point they may well visit you or communicate with you on a number of occasions before the final purchase. All these interactions have to be first class, because even though they may have chosen your business in their assessment, they can still back out if your handover is lacking.

If you can imagine some examples of when you personally received the following:

- A package through the post containing some goods that you ordered
- When you went to collect the car you'd paid for
- Paying a hotel bill
- Making a flight or holiday booking
- Buying a new computer, television or cooker

Did you end up getting exactly what you thought you would? This is not just about customer service, (which is generally, and genuinely, woefully lacking in most organisations), it's when you make your mind up whether the item or service you bought was worth the money, and whether you made the correct choice. Any dealings with you after signing the cheque, or making the reservation, or inputting a pin number, are verification points that they made the right decision.

A customer will be looking to see if you provide exactly what you promised. Just getting that one sale is not the ultimate objective, nor is it the end of the process if you want future sales. If you fail to do this you will lose credibility and future business through word of mouth. A key part of the marketing process therefore is to under-claim and over-deliver. Too many organisations over-claim and then under-deliver (most particularly government). It's a letdown and customers feel that *they* stupidly made the wrong purchase decision or that *their* assessment process was flawed.

An example from the 1980s, was a beautifully crafted television advertisement for British Rail, which aimed to promote rail travel by getting people out of their cars. It won a number of advertising awards, and showed a carriage full of people relaxing with their legs stretched out in total comfort and peace and quiet. The soundtrack was quite brilliant and the art direction was out of this world. However, the reality was all too often totally different. The ad succeeded in creating greater customer dissatisfaction because it clearly over-claimed and under-delivered, it just felt like an expensive ironic joke, with us as the customers the butt of the joke. Ironic that the advertising industry thought it was brilliant.

The times when a company really encourages positive word of mouth from me, is when I know exactly how much I have to pay, I get precisely what I thought I would when I thought I would get it, and they do something else on top of their marketing claims; something unexpected so that I'm pleasantly surprised. It's a talking point, and subconsciously enforces the fact that I have made a wise buying decision, so that I'm pretty pleased with myself.

I ordered a rather expensive case of wine through the internet the other month. It arrived on my doorstep *before* the expected delivery date, well-packaged with some tasting notes on why these wines were a good choice. There was also some newspaper reviews from a variety of wine critics and a very brief hand written note saying they hoped I enjoyed them. I truly thought that I had made a wise selection and that someone at the other end really cared about me as a customer. All it took was a couple of printed black and white sheets of paper and five seconds to write a note. It did make a difference to my interpretation of the company, and I would have no hesitation whatsoever in recommending them to anyone, which I have done. Dozens of times.

You have to do what it says on the tin and a bit more. You have to do things when you say you will or a bit before.

Access – in use 24 hours a day

Why is it that gas suppliers, delivery men, doctors *et al* think that I'm free between 9am and 5pm during the week? I'm sick of receiving little cards that tell me no-one was in when they came to take a meter reading, drop off a parcel or deliver a piece of furniture. And if I want to take some money out at 1.05pm on a Saturday at my building society, why are the doors steadfastly locked? (It's probably because they've been nationalized!). If I want an appointment at my doctors, why can I only get one in four weeks time on a Tuesday at 10.45am? Even our kids' school in Manchester is at it: *"Mrs Nelson, your daughter is ill, will you please come and pick her up at break time?"* Sorry mate, I'm in London at a meeting, did you think I was sitting at home knitting?

There's a terrible degree of arrogance about businesses or any other organisation who will only allow you access when it's convenient for them. They are also pretty stupid business people. The internet has changed our expectation of getting things, literally, on demand. You will do better if you recognise the changing pattern of working life and society in general. It sounds unbelievable but the 24/7 culture is fast becoming a reality.

At the moment at least 7 million people work between the hours of 6pm and 9am[101]. That's 1 in 7 UK adults. It's predicted to be 13 million (or a quarter of the population) by 2020. It's not surprising when most of us want to enjoy the fruits of our hard work, by eating out, shopping or socialising after we've finished work for the day. Smart businesses have cottoned on to that. They know they need to be there at that time to help me offload the money from my bank account after pay day. They also need to be there when the people who work those shifts have finished, or are about to start.

It's a circle that's self-perpetuating and it's not a trend set to diminish, between the hours of 6pm and 9am the following takes place:

- 15% of supermarket shopping (£32 billion a year)
- 69% of eating out
- 44% of household management (e.g. online banking, insurance, etc.) [102]

In fact, an amazing proportion of household management takes place between the hours of 4am and 9am, with call centres experiencing significant volumes in the very early morning. Mostly we can't make ourselves available 24 hours a day we just wouldn't make a profit, but we need to be mindful or our overall accessibility and have the flexible staffing teams to go with it.

---

[101] Future Foundation and MINT, (2003). *The Shape of Things to Come*
[102] Ibid

Another angle on accessibility is when you make the monumental decision to buy something, and then you cannot have it. You settle on a great new plasma screen television having read reviews, compared costs and talked to the sales guy in the shop. You go to pay and it's out of stock, or discontinued or you have to wait six weeks for it to be ordered. Or worse it actually costs much more because they haven't told you about the cables you need, or the pack of batteries for the remote or whatever. You need to include all information when someone is making the decision to use a service or buy a product of yours. You must manage expectations, over-deliver and be available as near to 24 hours a day as is practically feasible.

The whites of their eyes

You should try to do what it says on the tin, and make yourselves as available as possible, but if you don't do any of the things outlined in the Isaiah Logic process, you must just do this one thing above all else. It's what most owner/managers forget and it's the thing that everyone remembers without fail – customer service. For some reason it's never included in marketing texts and yet it's critical to business survival and healthy sales. It's the point when you actually deal with your customers and see the whites of their eyes, if only metaphorically speaking. It's what you've been waiting for, it's why you've spent all your marketing budget.

Customer service is the set of behaviours that an organisation undertakes during its interaction with customers. The notion that customer service was a tool to gain advantage over your competitors, really gained ground in the 1980s. Albrecht and Zemka[103] wrote that we live in a service dominated economy where organisations must perform as well as produce, and even physical products are distinguished by the quality of the service that goes with them. **Management gurus** started to talk about the customer driven business, with the slogan "Customer is King" evident on

---

[103] Albrecht, K., and Zemka, R. (1985), *Service America!*

office walls and the backs of delivery lorries. Not that anyone actually did anything about it – they just said it instead.

Jan Carlzon of Scandinavian Airlines claimed that he transformed his business by paying attention to what he called *Moments of Truth*[104]. Those subjective and fragmentary moments, when customers interacted with his company by phone or speaking to front line staff. He knew that was when they truly formed strong judgements about the company, whether good or bad.

Tom Peters (and others) grew to prominence by proclaiming the message that organisations need to be turned upside down to serve the customer. What he meant was that the standard organisational structure, where the importance and effort was at the top should be reversed, with attention, budget, training and status given to front-line customer contact employees. Some of that has sunk in, with most organisations claiming to treat customer satisfaction as an important issue. We have customer charters especially in government departments, hospitals and public transport. But unless your employees care or are trained and incentivised it will never happen. Customer expectations have increased, but so many businesses are terrible to deal with. Really terrible.

Most management commentators will outline the following to ensure great customer service:

Know your products or service offering

All your customer facing staff need to know your products or service offering inside out, availability, delivery, etc. and your complaints or returns policies to the letter. You must try to anticipate the types of questions customers will ask, even the stupid ones. I cannot count how many times I have gone into a shop or spoken to a supplier, and the person representing the organisation hasn't got the first clue. What do they get paid for? In a restaurant, how often have you asked what the 'soup of the day' is, and they don't know? Did they think no-one would ask? As previously discussed, you should not try to sell to prospective customers, you must try to give them

---

[104] Carlson, J. (1989), *Moments of Truth*

information so they can make comparisons and weigh up the options. Hard sell is a complete turn off for the huge majority of people, and if a customer eventually buys something you want them to come back, not be frightened away. Please don't train them to say, in that most accusatory of tones "can I help you?"

Treat people with courtesy and respect

Another infuriating thing is when you feel that you're doing the organisation a favour by being a customer. Or you feel you're an inconvenience to them, or you just get ignored. Every contact with a potential customer whether by e-mail, phone, written correspondence, or face-to-face leaves an impression. It's as much a part of corporate branding and style as your logo. If a member of staff is on a call and a customer is in front of them, you must train them to make eye contact and mouth "be with you in a minute", not ignore them. You must use phrases like "sorry to keep you waiting," "you're welcome," and "it's been a pleasure." And you must make sure they sound like they mean it.

Have a complaints policy

No matter how effective the service delivery process, things go wrong. Products have faults. Customers get frustrated. Staff make mistakes. Things slip through cracks. Obviously a customer is not always right. But instead of immediately focusing on what went wrong in a particular situation (you can have a good look at that later), you need to concentrate on how to fix it. The following statistics make for sober reading:

- It costs six times as more to attract a new customer as it does to keep an established one[105].
- 91% of unhappy customers will not willingly do business with you again[106].
- Customers quit for the following reasons – 1% die, 3% move

---

[105] The NACD Leadership Series
[106] Lee Resource Inc

away, 9% go to competitors, 14% because of product or service dissatisfaction, 68% because of indifferent staff attitudes[107].

- On average, for every customer who bothers to complain, 26 other customers remain silent, and even if they stay with you, it takes twelve positive service incidents to make up for one negative incident[108].
- 68% of customers are prepared to pay up to 20% more for good service[109].

Although the source is difficult to ascertain there is the customer service wives tale that 70% of customers will do business with you again if you resolve a complaint quickly and fairly. Even better, it's also claimed that 95% of dissatisfied customers will do business again if their complaint is resolved on the spot. This process, known as "recovery", is an important differentiator in building customer loyalty. Actively seek customer feedback and train staff how to handle customer complaints effectively using the correct mix of empathy, apology and resolution.

Focus on making customers, not making sales

Salespeople, especially those who get paid on commission, sometimes focus on volume sales instead of the quality of the sale. They need to realise that keeping a customer's business is more important than closing a sale. It's also cheaper.

Select the right people

When recruiting employees to provide customer service, the process often tends to concentrate more on functional expertise and experience, technical competence and knowledge rather than interpersonal skills. However, lack of the right attitude can drastically impact client satisfaction levels. Are your front line employees naturally smiley and do they genuinely 'like' people. You

---

[107] Leboeuf, Michael, *How To Win Customers And Keep Them For Life*, (2000)
[108] The Training Zone website, "Customer Service Statistics" (2006)
[109] ICS National Complaints Culture Survey (2006)

need to make sure they haven't got B.O., they look presentable and have the right attitude, you must also remember to develop, motivate and reward them too.

There are many books on customer service, and how to make it a priority if you want to steal customers from competitors and gain a legendary reputation. For me, it's not a separate function or process, but rather it's an important part of the whole marketing chain. But if you don't do insight research and work with customers to help design new products and services, it's no good having legendary service. After all, you could be the best producer of record players in the world and have a huge emphasis on customer facing activities in your shop, but if the world has moved on and they don't want them, you won't sell any.

Word of mouth

If getting noticed is more and more difficult, and customers are sceptical and aren't inclined to believe advertising claims, word of mouth becomes ever more important. Word of mouth is the passing of information by verbal means, and usually infers a recommendation. Typically it's considered a spoken communication, but it could be a web dialogue, such as a blog, message board, text or e-mail. This form of communication has a degree of credibility that cannot be achieved by mainstream advertising or promotion. People are more inclined to believe word of mouth promotion because the communicator is generally someone we know, and is unlikely to have an ulterior motive; they're not out to sell you something or make money out of you. This is confirmed by the Public Relations Society of America[110]:

> *"It has been said that word of mouth cannot be controlled, it can be managed and should not be ignored. The degree to which word-of-mouth communication occurs between family, friends, co-workers and neighbours is striking. Advice from family and friends is used by 43.7% of consumers when making purchase*

---

[110] *PR Tactics*, June 2007.

decisions, and nearly 25% follow advice from co-workers. Not surprisingly, credibility for both groups is high. The study suggests that consumers are looking for a more personalized touch when gathering information. They want to go to sources they know and can trust. Word-of-mouth communication encompasses these things."

Very successful word of mouth promotion creates a "buzz", which marketers are starting to try to recreate. Word of mouth is essentially a linear process with information passing from one individual to another, then to another, etc. You could almost track the sources and how they're passed on. But when there's a juicy rumour, a dramatic event, or an exciting new product, word of mouth intensifies and moves so quickly that the lines of communication almost form a matrix pattern rather than a linear one. Just think how you learnt about 9/11 or the London tube bombings. Word of mouth buzz was intense. Almost everyone in the country must have known about the horrible dramatic events within a few hours and yet most of us wouldn't have had access to a television or radio in that period. Obviously word of mouth is slower for the latest celebrity fling, and downright sluggish for a marketing promotion, but buzz can be achieved.

Positive word of mouth recommendation for your products or your services is the yardstick to measure how things are going. Not what your staff think, or your managers or your paymasters. If customers really like what you're doing, they will vote with their wallets or their purses. And if they recommend you to their friends, you've got it cracked. Sales figures are a sign of your current success, a good reputation spread by word of mouth will secure your future success.

Synopsis

Handover is when the potential customer has become a firm buyer, and takes possession of the product or service offered.

It's the opportunity to secure a good reputation through word of mouth and hence repeat or referred business.

Great handover leads to the most persuasive form of marketing – word of mouth. Yet despite the fact that word of mouth is the nirvana of marketing success, handover is the most neglected part of marketing. It involves convenient access and ready availability, customer service and complaint resolution. The key personnel are those that directly interface with the customer. If this part of the Isaiah Logic process is ignored the marketing budget, research, solution development and brand building are wasted and your reputation is in tatters. This is the time when the customer shapes their true opinion of your organisation, and you must do exactly what you promised. If not, word of mouth will out-do any marketing attempt (no matter what the budget) to correct popular opinion.

HOW TO DELIVER GREAT HANDOVER

Where to get the best

Obviously this element is about great customer service and includes topics that relate and overlap with 'assessment' (above). Staff that come into contact with your customers during any part of this process need to be trained, with scenarios developed, to empower them to make decisions when faced with customer complaints or problems.

There are off-the-peg programmes which not only include customer service training but managing conflict and dealing with difficult people. If your company is large enough there should be a formalised personnel development structure, linked to performance reviews or appraisal targets, possibly with an incentivised bonus element. Alternatively a training company can work with the management team to develop a bespoke package, to cover all the areas you need specifically geared to your organisation and its industry sector.

On a budget

Off-the-peg training modules for customer service can be cost effective, but if your budget cannot run to such an expense, you could develop team away days to concentrate on how you can better serve your customers. Walk your team out of the building, get them to walk back in and observe everything as if they were a customer. Encourage them to develop processes they believe will make your business world class, get them to put themselves in the position of the customer. Ask them to give examples of first hand experiences of poor customer service – how did it make them feel? There is a book called *The Big Book of Customer Service Training*

Games[111] which might help.

Other possibilities include implementing a timetable of mystery shops that staff conduct internally on a rota basis, but make sure they report their findings back to the team. Or you could initiate an 'employee of the month' scheme, with cash or prizes awarded.

Where to find customer service training

Further Education Colleges provide NVQs in customer service if you want to put your staff through a structured programme that will lead to a nationally recognised qualification. These are work-related and competency based. To find your nearest course go to www.hotcourses.com and use the search facility by selecting your location and typing in "customer service".

Learn Direct as part of the University for Industry was set up by government to provide high quality learning and training. They have an online course called "Steps to Success: Professional Customer Service", which costs around £70. It uses video and interactive exercises for effective communication, building a loyal customer base and dealing efficiently with customer problems. By going on to their website at www.learndirect-business.co.uk, you can pay online and be up and running in a matter of minutes.

Recommended further reading

- Blanchard, K., Bowles, S. (1998), *Raving Fans: Revolutionary Approach to Customer Service*
- Heppell, M. (2006), *Five Star Service, One Star Budget: How to Create Magic Moments for Your Customers That Get You Noticed, Remembered and Referred*

---

[111] Carlaw, P., Demming, V.K., (2006), *The Big Book of Customer Service Training Games: Quick, Fun Activities for All Customer Facing Employees*

THAT'S THE WAY TO DO IT

Real life handover examples

Google

Google began in January 1996 as a research project by Larry Page, a Ph.D. student at Stanford University in America. Whilst looking for a dissertation theme, he decided to explore the mathematical properties of the World Wide Web, trying to depict its structure as a huge graph. He was joined by fellow student and friend Sergey Brin, and used a web crawler from his university home page as its starting point. Page and Brin converted the data it gathered into a PageRank algorithm, which consisted of a list of returned links ranked by web page importance. In the process it occurred to them that a search engine based on PageRank would produce better results than existing techniques, which at the time essentially ranked results according to how many times the search term appeared on a page.

The research convinced Page and Brin that the web pages with the most links to them from other highly related pages, would be the most relevant sites associated with an internet search. Page and Brin tested their thesis as part of their studies, and laid the foundation for their search engine. Originally they used the Stanford University website with the domain name as www.google.stanford.edu. The domain *google.com* was registered in 1997 and a year later Google Inc was formally incorporated at a friend's garage in California. The name "Google" originated from a misspelling of googol which refers to the number represented by a 1 followed by one-hundred zeros.

By the end of 1998, Google had an index of about 60 million pages. The home page was still marked "alpha test", but an article argued that its search results were technically superior and better than those viewed by stock market investors as "the future of the web", such as Yahoo!, Hotbot, Lycos, Netcentre and MSN. Other commentators soon agreed and a year later Google Inc moved into new offices in Silicon Valley, finally settling into the complex which has since become known as the Googleplex.

The Google search engine attracted a loyal following among the growing number of Internet users, who liked its simple design, and in 2000 they began selling advertisements associated with search keywords. However the ads remained text-based to maintain the uncluttered page design and to maximize page loading speed.

The Google company culture has been strongly held by Page and Brin despite the company's spectacular growth. They declared the organisation's code of conduct as "don't be evil", declaring "we believe strongly that in the long term, we will be better served – as shareholders and in all other ways – by a company that does good things for the world even if we forgo some short term gains."

Another key company commitment is to focus on the user, they state "focus on the user and all else will follow. From its inception, Google has focused on providing the best user experience possible. While many companies claim to put their customers first, few are able to resist the temptation to make small sacrifices to increase shareholder value. Google has steadfastly refused to make any changes that does not offer a benefit to the users who come to the site."

Google has appeared as the top "Most Loved" brand in the UK by some margin over the last couple of years. For 2007 it took 69% share of the total vote[112]. Those that are high up the list tend to be aspirational brands, that forge a strong connection with their customers and are highly engaging. Great customer service, authenticity and trust are key to popularity and corresponding sales.

---

[112] *Marketing's* Brands We Love and Hate survey, in association with Joshua G2.

By autumn 2007 Google hit, what was then, an all time market value of over $200 billion, more than News Corp, Disney, Viacom and CBS combined. The valuation made Google the second largest technology company in the world, behind Microsoft.

Brin, the company's President of Technology, and Page, President of Products, take an annual salary of $1 each, but they both hold around $13 billion in Google shares.

THAT'S THE WAY TO DO IT

Real life handover examples

Le Manoir aux Quat'Saisons

I booked *Le Manoir aux Quat'Saisons* for our 25th wedding anniversary. A lot of money and a lot of expectation, considering Le Manoir has held two Michelin stars for 23 years, won numerous awards, featured in all the best hotel and restaurant guides and Raymond Blanc appears on television espousing the virtues of excellent customer service. Was he over promising and under delivering?

We arrived in the October pouring rain, and as soon as we drew up a member of staff rushed out and escorted us under his umbrella to the reception door. He insisted he take the car keys, emptied our boot of suitcases, delivered them to our room and drove the car to its allotted space. Meanwhile the receptionist knew our name (how?) and personally escorted us to our room, merrily explaining the various features of the grounds and the rest of the hotel. As we settled in, some homemade cake and a fresh cup of properly brewed tea was delivered.

The bathroom was spotless, the pillows plump, the furnishings stylish. I thought I spotted a flaw when there was obviously no tea or coffee making facilities. However, we were asked when we wanted morning tea and ordered it for 8am. The dinner was sublime, the staff friendly, efficient and very knowledgeable. The next morning? At two minutes to eight, a phone call asked if we were ready for our morning tea. At exactly 8 a knock on the door confirmed its arrival.

It cost a lot of money, but they made it feel worth it and there were no surprises on the bill. We're saving up for our next visit, and I've told so many people about our experience they probably need never advertise again.

THAT'S THE WAY TO DO IT

Real life handover examples

Enterprise Rent-a-Car

Enterprise Rent-A-Car is the number one rental car company in North America. Jack Taylor founded Enterprise in 1957 as a privately-owned business. In the UK and Ireland, Enterprise has won many awards including:

- Best Corporate Car Rental Company – Institute of Transport Management
- Top 50 'Where women want to work' – The Times with Aurora
- O2 Ability Awards
- Service Provider of the Year – British Insurance Awards
- Best Graduate Advert and Best Graduate Web Site – Recruitment Advertising awards

So how do they do it? The aim of the company is to "exceed customer expectations", not give shareholder value, increase profits or market share. That's it. So many mangers moan that you can change business and structures, but to change culture takes forever. In some ways this is not strictly true. If you have firm commitment at the top and through the executive ranks, you can change culture if you really, really want to. In the case of Enterprise, they did this by aligning the overall aim and vision with their measurement and incentive framework. That is to say – keep customers happy and you will prosper in the company. No one is in any doubt that the key measure for every member of staff, be it managerial or administrative, is to exceed customer expectations. This is unusual because most appraisals and rewards are about increased profits or sales, but Enterprise firmly believe that if a customer is happy those things will automatically follow, not the other way around.

So Enterprise directors created a questionnaire for customers based on just two questions to verify the key measure, which let's face it, are the most pertinent:

1. How would you rate your last Enterprise experience?
2. Would you rent from Enterprise again?

This makes a change because most customer surveys are far too long, and consequently the response rate is low. But this approach has ensured that the opposite is true in this case. The results of the survey form part of the Enterprise Service Quality Index – the basis for measuring performance of the various rental branches of Enterprise.

This illustrates that Enterprise is not really a car rental business at all. It does hire cars, but its main concern is keeping the customer happy and exceeding their expectations. That's why Forbes currently ranks the company as number 16 in the top 100 private companies in the US.

Sales jumped by 25% compared with an equivalent period before the implementation of the new design[113]. HMV decided to roll out key elements of the new design across its existing stores, as well as its new developments in the Liverpool One and Westfield London shopping centres.

DON'T TRY THIS AT HOME

Marketing disasters – handover

Fridge delivery

If you order a pizza by phone, it's pretty obvious that when the spotty teenager on the moped arrives 15 minutes later, you will be in. But if you look at all the literature and then turn up at an out-of-town store to buy the fridge you like the look of, what happens when you discuss the delivery bit? You clearly can't fit it in your Fiat 500/Jaguar/Mini. You've surfed the internet or whatever and have found the fridge you want has 50% off and the total cost is now £100. Brilliant – a bargain. But when you discuss delivery it's only "during office hours", which generally means, when you're at work. You discuss it between you and clearly someone has to take a day off. But if you earn £26,000, (taking into account there are 260 working days a year), a day off actually costs £100. If you earn £50k a year, you're talking £192. That fridge is looking awfully expensive, but is that how the seller sees it? No, of course not.

Not only do they organise their deliveries when no-one is in, they can't even tell you when they will be there. If you're lucky it will be a choice between afternoon or morning. But

---

[113] Design Council, 23 December 2008

when you try to get a definition of what that means, it's terribly elusive: "Will it be from 8am or 9 in the morning? And what about the afternoon? Is that midday or 1pm?" They reply: "Sorry, mate can't give you any definitive answers because it depends on the delivery route, and they are sub-contractors, they don't actually work for us directly." So you ask: "What is the delivery route, am I in the middle, at the beginning or the end?" "I don't know, we can't give it to you." Feeling ever more exasperated you ask: "Even that morning, when the guys start work, could they just give me a call and let me know, once they've got their route finalised, where I will roughly be in the overall schedule?" The obvious answer to that is: "No."

Once I realised the real price of buying white goods i.e. the great discounted selling price, and then the additional cost of me waiting for delivery, I started to look for retailers that deliver when it was convenient for me and not convenient for them. Although they might be a little bit more expensive, in real terms they weren't. Surely it can't be that long before more consumers cotton on to this fact?

DON'T TRY THIS AT HOME

Marketing disasters – handover

Call centres

Most of us have insurance policies or bank accounts with large companies based in the UK. We are seduced by the advertising premise, or the latest product offering they have. Of course, once hooked, it's terribly difficult to remove ourselves. Changing your car insurance once it's already been bought, or worse, changing your bank account and all your direct debits and so on, is a dreadful nuisance. But why would you move your business and what would prompt you to complain so vociferously?

You might carry out a price comparison and feel you can get a better deal elsewhere. But more often than not, it's poor customer service. The banks in particular, have been very quick to save money by closing small, apparently unprofitable, branches, and replace face to face interaction with call centres. In essence, they were open for longer hours than the branches, but have the executives who insisted on this strategy ever used one? Most of us with a problem, just get to the point where no-one seems to want to listen, you can't make any progress and there is generally a lack of will to genuinely help you. If that is, you can get through in the first place.

From the turn of this century, companies such as Norwich Union (now Aviva) have been enthusiastically off shoring their call centre operations, with some claiming they had saved as much as 75% on UK provision. It's the sort of strategy that has got the banks and insurance companies into meltdown hell, as they strive for financial gains, without considering the impact on customers. According to research by *The Financial Mail on Sunday* and *This is Money*[114], call centres remain one of the most hated aspects of dealing with banks and other companies, especially those based abroad. Most people vehemently deny this is a matter of xenophobia or racism, just that they want someone to understand their problems and deal with them sympathetically and quickly.

Delays in answering, incomprehensible accents, mispronounced names and lack of familiarity with UK geography were the most common hates. Customers were generally annoyed because the operators "don't know what the customer is talking about"[115]. One respondent told of a

[114] "We all hate talking to India", *Mail on Sunday*, 12 February 2006
[115] Aviva spokeswoman – "Norwich Union call centre U-turn", 28 January 2007, *Financial Mail on Sunday*

call centre employee who thought Cardiff was in the West Midlands, another that they couldn't make the person understand that their immersion heater had broken down and caused a flood, because they didn't know what an immersion heater was. Another Asia-based worker confused Birmingham UK, with the American town in Alabama. Most people also suspected that Asia-based workers who claimed they had English names such as Edward or Geraldine were lying, which they disliked. 95% of respondents said foreign call centres were a pet hate and they would like to ditch service providers that developed them. 69% said such service was consistently poor. In the research the poorest call centre service was delivered by Dell, BT, HSBC and Norwich Union.

In 2005 Abbey National closed all its Indian call centres, bringing 1,000 jobs back to Britain following a huge number of complaints. Powergen moved all its call centre operations back in 2006 after five years, again following complaints from customers, as well as a decision that it would be easier to manage and train staff in the UK[116]. Norwich Union moved its call centre work back to the UK, which cost 150 jobs in India. Other services moved back to Britain include credit hire and executive pension schemes. Aviva admitted that when Norwich Union started transferring thousands of jobs to India, it did not consider such cultural difficulties.

---

[116] "Powergen closes Indian call centres", 15 June 2006, *This is Money*

PART 9

A NEW DEFINITION FOR A NEW WORLD

A DEFINITION OF MARKETING

So what *is* marketing then?

There are hundreds of definitions of marketing, but usually the official representative bodies would give the definitive answer:

"Marketing is the management process responsible for identifying, anticipating and satisfying customer requirements profitably."[117]

"Marketing is an organizational function and a set of processes for creating, communicating, and delivering value to customers and for managing customer relationships in ways that benefit the organization and its stakeholders."[118]

The first is the Chartered Institute of Marketing's definition. Their website states that the CIM is "the leading international body for marketing and business development". Each year they help over 50,000 people "at every stage of their career with training, qualifications and resources as well as enabling leading businesses to get the most from their marketing people." They can confer someone who has gone through their training, (or is an experienced practitioner) as a Chartered Marketer. And yet they still use, and endorse, the outdated and potentially damaging Four Ps methodology in their training.

At this moment in time they have admitted that "the role of marketing . . . has changed in the 30 years since The Institute last defined (it)." They are acutely aware that it no longer fits and have said they want a debate about the marketing process and a marketing definition amongst the industry – quite right too. Surely it would make sense to adapt the Isaiah methodology.

---

[117] The Chartered Institute of Marketing – UK (2003)
[118] The American Marketing Association (2005)

If you've read this process and still believe the official definitions are a reflection of a rapidly evolving new century, my arguments have failed. For me, my personal experience and common sense don't subscribe to those points of view, they don't feel appropriate or real. They won't help you achieve the ultimate marketing goal of sustainable new business and record sales figures, by keeping existing customers happy, and making new ones through positive word of mouth recommendation. If you are a charity or public sector body they won't help you get your message across, influence partners and stakeholders or win over new supporters. In any organisation, they won't gain you a fantastic reputation.

Organisations who start to seek out marketing expertise, generally feel they need more business, customers, supporters, shareholder value, profit or turnover. Put bluntly they're either heading in a new direction, going for growth or are in trouble. They then employ a marketing professional and expect them to attain the corporate results they desperately desire, almost immediately.

But marketing is not carried out by one person or one department. I think Drucker's[119] definition is the closest:

"(Marketing) encompasses the entire business. It's the whole business seen   from the point of view of its final result, that is, from the customer's point of view."

My definition is very similar:

"Marketing is a philosophy not a process. It's about putting the customer at the centre of every business decision you make. It's about gaining and keeping a positive, word of mouth reputation."

And therefore my definition of a marketer is:

"A person in the organisation that champions, safeguards and represents the views of customers, ensuring all business decisions and processes are made for their convenience."

---

[119] Drucker, P.F. (1954), *The Practice of Management*

In both these definitions, the customer is the intended end audience – whether they are a stakeholder, buyer, influencer, advocate or partner.

Logical marketing for practical people is hard and difficult. It means you have to make advocates out of all of your staff, and you have to personally lead from the front and insist on a new way of thinking. If you just want incremental gains and short term results and don't care about your customers, there are lots of ways of getting them, just ask the High Street banks. You can set a number of those in motion now. To get some quick but temporary wins – just slash your prices, or go for a big budget advertising campaign that in all honesty doesn't reflect what the reality of your product or service really is. That may get you a first purchase, but probably not a repeat one. If you want real profits and sustained competitive advantage especially in tough times, you need permanently happy customers who honestly believe you have a great reputation, and are willing to recommend you by word of mouth.

Truly putting customers first is a philosophy, and it should be right up there in your vision, mission and your corporate planning. You can't pretend outwardly, but actually dismiss it behind closed doors, you have to fundamentally believe it, not just with your business head, but with all your heart, and you have to lead your staff through it.

If you do, Isaiah Logic is offered as a roadmap to achieve an outstanding business reputation with genuine long term success. If you don't . . . ultimately this process is useless, but you can get some short term unsustainable gains, by pulling the wool over your customers' eyes, if you want to risk it.

PART 10

SOME PREDICTIONS

THE FUTURE OF MARKETING

The arrival of a different age has undoubtedly shown up the defects in the Four P methodology, with loud cries for a new model to replace it. There has been a huge technological shift in the marketing and communications landscape for some time, but now it has been coupled with severe and profound changes in the economics of business and our trust and attitude in once-stable and powerful institutions.

It is always difficult to predict the future with any certainty, but there are clearly key themes emerging that will affect approaches to marketing, and every single one results in more power to the customer not less. The days of sticking an ad on television and waiting for the sales to roll in, are well and truly gone. This makes the need for a customer-centric marketing approach critical, and you could (should) argue that it means a customer-centric whole business approach as well.

The Isaiah methodology is important today, but it's going to be essential in the future. The process explains new marketing elements described as "information gathering" and "assessment". These will become accepted as legitimate steps in the marketing process rather than the add-ons they are today, as an even more dramatic shift to 'reverse markets' takes place. That is, multiple markets and entry points where the customer seeks out a supplier/provider when they are ready, not markets as physical places where suppliers and providers seek out customers and try to sell them as many products/services as possible. Potential buyers will want more access to information before they can make an assessment.

The likely key themes that will dramatically impact marketing in the future are shown below, although not in any particular order of preference. If you can be prepared for them, you will be one step ahead of your competitors and probably your customers too.

Develop strategies to combat attention scarcity

We are all bombarded by thousands of advertising messages a day – advertising hoardings, vehicle livery, street sellers, internet banners, e-mail spam, radio, magazine, newspaper and television advertising ad infinitum. In retaliation we have developed scarce attention spans and block out things that are not of immediate interest to us. Businesses that focus purely on attention getting as their marketing strategy, are desperate to gain airtime – to stop us in our tracks and to intrude in our space they are using increasingly invasive tactics – pop up ads on internet sites, messages projected on the sides of buildings, plastered on the sides of farm animals in fields, in between the overs of a thrilling cricket match (no irony intended at all) and running on video displays above urinals. You can't even walk down the high street without someone accosting you for something. Some days I just want to scream "LEAVE ME ALONE" and I work in marketing. These tactics are having the opposite affect for the companies that are most intrusive. Some I have vowed never ever to use, even if I don't know what their product or service is like, purely because they annoy me. It's the equivalent of the aggressive "can I help you" as soon as you set foot through the door of a shop.

Rather than just focusing on how to get attention and risk turning prospective buyers off, businesses need to consider how they can help their customers receive notification of the things that actually are important to them. Acting as a filter in this way, is similar to being an internet portal or hub that signposts interested parties to the destinations that matter to them. It shortcuts the process, saves time, builds loyalty and acts as a genuine and valuable service.

Businesses have been commoditising awareness activities, viewing attention seeking as a single activity aligned to a product, service or message that is being sold. They have been pushing and thrusting things outwards to potential customers, not working from the customer viewpoint and enticing them in. Shooting not fishing. For anyone walking down the street or surfing the internet, awareness raising (in any form) simply cuts across the context of what they are currently doing or thinking. Gaining attention is highly context sensitive – it is intensely personal and social at the same time. It is also deeply embedded in, and shaped by, relationships, which are far from static, but increasingly dynamic.

Organisations need to think from the customers point of view – what will help them, what will genuinely be of interest, how can we build mutually beneficial relationships? The mindset has to change and the key challenge and opportunity for businesses in the future will be how to participate in, and enrich these relationships in order to amplify the value of attention and become more significant to their customers.

Aim for one-to-one marketing

With increasing power and choice, customers want to be fêted. They will want their status recognised and will expect customisation. They won't want the rigidity of going into a restaurant and being told that they can't have the starter from one menu and the main course from another. Or they can have this computer bundle, but it has to be with that make of printer, not the one they actually want. Just think of the example of BMW's mini (a long way from "any colour as long as it's black"), you can get hundreds of variations of the car, just as you can buy an almost infinite number of coffee variations from Starbucks. Customers are getting used to it, and will want almost one-to-one marketing, or at least the perception of it.

Businesses will need to get into co-creating products with customers, or allowing that possibility. It will require a "many to one" mindset. The winners in the future will be organisations that can mobilise a number of networks or resources, and cleverly orchestrate the ability to create almost bespoke customisations whilst keeping a reasonable cost base.

Understand the irony of 'local' in a global context

Food, fuel and energy security are issues that are progressively finding themselves at the forefront of disaster planning. The government has plans and counter measures to defend us from a number of nightmare scenarios. But mitigation plans aren't just about protecting today's social infrastructure, but designing and planning new build and community growth that minimise future threats. One of the most fragile distribution systems which is probably the easiest to disrupt is the food chain. We might be able to live without fuel and energy for a while (although we hate giving up our cars), but panic sets in very early if we don't have food.

The supermarkets have grown to such an extent that they not only operate large out of town and high street positions, but have taken over the role of the corner shop too, muscling out independent local stores with a distinct lack of grace. Our dependency on the supermarket chains to provide us with full shelves of food available almost 24 hours a day, gives rise to a complacent feeling that food will always be available. But these multi-million pound businesses have almost no stock at all; it takes up space which costs money and eats into the retail area. Instead, deliveries happen practically every minute which gives the illusion of constant 'backroom' supplies. They have developed a hugely sophisticated distribution system, where the intricacies of logistics and *just in time* processes are paramount. There are precious little reserves of food to sustain any protracted interruption (we're talking days not weeks), whether this is through terrorism, fuel shortages or extreme weather conditions.

We export food we produce in the UK to other countries, whilst at the same time importing the same foodstuff for our own consumption. For example, Britain imports 61,400 tonnes of poultry meat a year from the Netherlands and exports 33,100 tonnes to the Netherlands[120]. Similarly, in the unlikely event that a foodstuff is produced 5 miles from your front door, and sold in your local supermarket, it is more likely to be transported first to the distribution hub which could be hundreds of miles away, before it is delivered to the shop down your road at its precisely allocated time slot.

---

[120] Caroline Lucas, C. (2001) "Stopping the Great Food Swap – Relocalising Europe's food supply", Green Party, 2001.

MI5 apparently uses the "four meals" rule to assess the threat levels from attacks on strategic installations, such as computer networks and power stations, natural disasters, widespread strikes and civil disobedience[121]. They believe that after as little as four missed meals, a "law of the jungle" would take over, in which citizens would resort to looting and violence to find food with a consequent breakdown of civil order. We've found ourselves in a position where logistics have become illogistical.

No wonder, governments and the public are increasingly worried about the impact of global warming, security and unforeseen disasters that would affect the current distribution of food. For this reason there are real signs that the process inherent in food supply and distribution as well as other industries could be reversed by re-establishing local and regional supply systems and substituting 'near for far' production and distribution. This would reduce both the demand for, and the environmental burdens associated with, transportation and give greater national security and local independence. Planners are beginning to look at locally generated power for new housing developments for the same reasons.

It is therefore quite likely that towns, cities and villages will slowly begin to return to more sustainable independent communities with an emphasis on local delivery and production where possible. This is ironic given the dependence we all have on the global reach of the internet and the international nature of our transactions.

In the future, many businesses will need to work out how their communications and marketing activity can be accessed globally, but their products and services sourced locally or reflect local sensitivities.

Predict customer action, reaction and behaviours

To truly understand customers; how they want customisation to be organised, how they want 'local but global' to manifest itself and

---

[121] *The Times* (10 October 2004) "Four Meals Away From Anarchy".

how their attention can positively gained, insight will become ever more important. Businesses and their products and services, will become valuable in this new marketing world if they offer a very different customer-centric promise. It won't be "buy from me because I have the best" whatever, it will be "buy from me because I know you as an individual customer better than anyone and you can trust me to use that knowledge to construct the right product and service solution to meet your individual needs."

Marketing strategies and business processes will need to be reshaped along these lines and more of the budget allocated to insight to really get inside the minds of customers. Developing solutions for them, with either new or revised products and services, will be almost unthinkable without this type of research. Those businesses that do are likely to be richly rewarded.

In the public sector, research into behaviours has become more embedded, especially in the NHS, as they desperately try to get across health messages on obesity, smoking, sexual health, drug and alcohol addiction. Often these are particularly relevant to the most deprived and hard to engage audiences, and without insight into behaviours and attitudes, these campaigns have no chance of success. You can't just tell people what to do anymore – communications that simply state "stop smoking" or "keep Britain tidy" have no resonance. Messages have to be engaging and finely geared to the target audience. The Department of Health has strongly advocated insight investment before budgets are allocated for community campaigns. It will not be long before other government departments responsible for engaging the public to voluntarily participate in initiatives such as recycling, see the value of this approach and follow suit.

Focus on real customer service

Many decades ago the vendor had more power, and customers were deferential towards big business and particularly the institutions. There were less organisations offering far fewer products and services, and the lead time involved in copying a competitor was much longer. Now as soon as a successful product or service innovation hits the market, it is almost immediately copied. This leads to a huge proliferation of business models, products and services, and there are very few monopolies. Customer choice is almost infinite and customer loyalty rare. So if all coffee shops, opticians, window cleaners, computers are very similar especially in price, there is only one remaining differentiator – customer service. This doesn't apply when a new innovation hits the market, but as soon as that market matures because by that time, first mover advantages that allow premium pricing are lost. Once again it boils down to treating your customers better than the competition.

The systematic and significant decline in interaction costs makes it easier for customers to identify sellers, find information about them, negotiate with them, monitor their performance and switch from one to another if they're not satisfied with performance. Customer service is crucial and more so in the future, and if you think you can get away without training your staff to excel in this area, or if you employ the wrong front line people who can't be bothered, it will affect your income especially in the area of repeat sales. Businesses will have to prioritise and focus more budget on the elements of business that interface with customers, rather than leaving it as an afterthought.

Demand marketing authenticity

Being honest and managing expectations is a key theme of this book. Marketing is about keeping customers, not just making sales. For long term success you have to be authentic. As stated a number of times, if you try to dupe your customers they will find out. Not necessarily now, but very soon. Companies that think their customers are stupid by treating them badly or misleading them, will face catastrophic failure at some point, it's just a matter of when. Pretending a product can do something it can't, making it impossible to lodge a genuine complaint, publicising a price which really cannot be achieved after all the obligatory add-ons, offering a service which you can't get immediately even though you've paid for it. Do you think customers don't notice? Do you think they don't tell other people how they have been conned? Do you think they will use you again? It's a recipe for diminishing returns.

Another, not so obvious example are those marketing departments (and politicians for that matter) that set up blogs, wikis, virtual communities and social networks, treating them like a checklist to be deployed so they can appear cool. At least it means they can say to the MD, who doesn't know what they are anyway; "yes, don't worry we've set up some blogs." In some cases they pretend their own staff are customers, or get one of the junior staff or a PR to write the MD's blog for them. But when you're exposed, where does that leave you?

Marketing authenticity is another essential tool post credit crunch. Consumers are now very sensitive to any company that attempts to pull the wool over their eyes, and with social networks in the hands of the customer, they'll let everyone know about it.

Measure and protect your reputation

Business reputation is established by gaining and retaining the confidence and trust of the stakeholders in the business: customers, suppliers and employees, as well as shareholders, funding partners and Board members. Reputation is gained over time, sometimes very quickly when a new operation is launched, but more frequently, over the longer term by maintaining the trust and confidence of a range of stakeholders. Business reputations are hard to win but quickly lost either by poor handling of a major corporate crisis or more commonly, through lacklustre management or customer service. The first can hit the bottom line very quickly (think Ratner and "crap" jewellery), but the second is usually shown by a slow steady decline in sales.

Reputational risk is inherent in all risks whether they are financial, strategic, regulatory or operational. At the end, if an organisation has a very poor reputation, eventually it will cease to trade. A good reputation can be manipulated and managed; even corporate disasters if handled well, can lead to increased business. Trust and consumer confidence are key, but it can no longer be achieved through big advertising or promotional campaigns. Consumers are more cynical than ever about marketing claims, and have access to product and service reports at a touch of a button through the internet. Word of mouth is the key marketing tool. As far as customers are concerned, their belief in your reputation (your organisation) is based on expectations versus experience: **belief** (what an organisation does and how it delivers) informs our **expectation** (about how an organisation would behave in a certain situation) against which we measure our **experience** of how it actually performed or engaged.

For high performing organisations it is seen as the most critical risk, because reputation is becoming a key source of competitive advantage as products and services become less differentiated. It is the one risk for which CEOs have direct and individual responsibility, though many other risks have reputational elements embedded in them. In a recent survey by the Economist Intelligence Unit[122], it emerged as the highest ranking priority (52%) above regulatory (41%) and human capital (41%) risks.

Increased governance, legal and regulatory influences have made companies more vulnerable to reputational damage. However, the real threat to reputation is the power and intrusiveness of the media, and most especially the rise of internet blogging and "citizen's journalism" which feeds directly into the hands of journalists looking to generate bad news stories. The public rely on such reporting to form their expectation of a product or service.

Strong corporate brands, identities and reputations are being

---

[122] January 2006; Reputational Risk

progressively linked with improvements in financial performance. They are increasingly being treated as significant intangible assets, sometimes worth up to twice the book value of their tangible assets[123]. There is also emerging empirical proof of a strong and positive link between corporate reputation and financial performance[124]. The basis for both of these financial outcomes – improved book market values and sustained profitability – arise from the ability of companies to *differentiate* themselves in the marketplace precisely because intangible assets are difficult to copy[125]. For example it is possible to replicate the food and accommodation at Le Manoir, but to replicate their management style, image and service delivery is much more difficult.

Reputations and brands have more value when an organisation has *relative* advantages over others. Therefore the true, longer term differentiator against the competition, is not "me too" models of organisational efficiency or corporate social responsibility statements, (which should be the socially accepted norm), but a strong reputation based on cultural behaviour through customer service, that does not incur a public perception penalty for being too different[126].

But how can you manipulate reputation? Below are the key elements that constitute reputation[127]:

- **Innovation and vision** – emotional appeal
- **Financial soundness and performance** – long term investment value, financial transparency and regulatory compliance
- **Efficient systems and operations** – including financial efficiency but built backwards from customer needs and wants
- **External corporate social responsibility** – treatment of

---

[123] Hatch & Schultz, 2001; Fombrun & Van Riel, 2003; Fombrun, 2005.
[124] Deephouse & Carter, 2005; Roberts and Dowling, 2002.
[125] Fombrun & Van Riel, 2003.
[126] Deephouse & Carter, 2005
[127] Taken from the annual "Most Admired Companies", *Management Today/Fortune* and "Reputation Quotient", *Financial Times*

workers, workplace environment, ethical use of corporate assets and open community responsibility
- **Quality of products or services** – including value for money
- **Quality of management and leadership** – developing people excellence, stakeholder relationships and good crisis management
- **Employee talent and culture** – superior customer service and delivering customer promise
- **Brand, image and identity** – consistent branding/messaging aligned to leadership, management and employee behaviour, responsible marketing and leveraging of marketing spend

If the banks had concentrated on authenticity in their marketing and valued reputation, I honestly don't think they would be in the mess they are now. Explaining, in plain English, the investment or borrowing choices a customer has, and the real risks involved should be a relatively easy task. After all, if you can't explain it, there must be something wrong. Dreaming up ever complicated ways of extracting money from people who can't afford it, because the company's incentive and career path rewards you for doing so, feels immoral and somehow dishonest. Our trust in them is so low, their focus on personal gain so exposed, we've had to take ownership of the company away from them.

Reputation is likely to be a key measure for future business performance, it is intimately related to authenticity and customer service. To make it happen in your business, you need to believe this is so, both with your heart and your head, making sure your staff do too. As shown in the Isaiah Model, reward and promote those people that have the ability to turn customers into advocates.

Acknowledge grey market prominence

Whilst the media, films, music and the entertainment industry relentlessly focus on youth and technology, the plain fact is the population is aging dramatically. There are already more people over 60 years old than those aged 0-14. We may picture that age range as old and frail, scrapping an existence on a small state pension, but the facts contradict that perception:

- As much as 40% (£260bn) of total UK annual consumer spending can be attributed to the over 50s
- In 2003/4 UK households headed by someone aged 50-64 spent on average £441 per week
- People aged 50-65 spend twice as much on leisure and entertainment as the under-30s
- The over 50s buy 80% of all top of the range cars, 50% of skincare products and 80% of leisure cruises
- 56% of the 50+ population have a home pc or laptop
- 70% have a mobile phone and 46% access to digital TV[128]

It has been widely written that the average age for purchasing a Harley Davidson is now 59!

The over 50s (those classified as 'grey') are post-war baby boomers of the 60s and 70s – the trail blazers of the consumer generation and youth culture, so it shouldn't be surprising that official music industry statistics, show the over-60s spending as much on music as 12 – 19 year olds, while 50 – 59 year olds spend almost the same as those in their twenties.

However, brand managers and agency executives are normally in their 20s and 30s and do not recognise the power of the 'grey pound', often advocating marketing strategies and promotions which exclude this highly lucrative market. Organisations need to recognise that the over 50s enjoy lives that are every bit as full and energetic as younger people, and they have the time to weigh up purchasing decisions. Make sure your marketing strategy actively targets this group.

Today's greys include Madonna, Kim Bassinger, Sharon Stone, Pierce Brosnan, Liam Neeson and Bruce Willis. Perhaps we should rethink the term "grey"?

---

[128] Age Concern

Understand the post-modern context

For most of us today there are almost no hierarchical dimensions to consider as past generations have. We may still have a thinly veiled class system, but it really is nothing like it was. Growing up in the 1950's, it was very clear that 'the establishment' dictated much of work and home life, the media, sport and so on. Laws dictated a somewhat suppressed society, especially in relation to sex. The old order meant institutions and governments filled with middle-aged, Oxbridge educated white men with cut glass BBC accents, dominating every area of decision making in the private and public sectors. The general population couldn't access things instantly, they didn't really get their voice heard or have much consumer choice. They had to save and plan and wait.

Now many things are available this minute, on demand, right now. Witness the growth of text messaging, credit card bills, fast food and multi-tv channels. In today's fast-paced ever-changing world, the general population has much of the power, with 'the establishment' rarely quoted as existing, let alone dictating lifestyles. Ordinary people have more money, and in the battle of the brands consumers have the ultimate power of choice, and those choices are almost limitless. News moves instantly too, and is available 24 hours a day. If an issue breeds some form of rebellion, the media quickly commoditises it and makes it seem mainstream. Difficult to feel rebellious when that happens. Anyhow with so much freedom and choice, so much you can access this second – what 'real issues' could you reasonably rebel against?

Post-modernism means there is no easily determined structure; so many topics and themes have equal 'air time'. The march of popular culture, which is determined by consumer whim, is increasingly superficial and short-lived. We are all used to news, music, fads, celebrities and fashions that come and go very quickly, with weighty, globally-important issues being juxtapositioned against frivolous, puerile ones. Witness the war in Iraq reported in the same breath as Victoria Beckham's attempt at a musical comeback.

This new culture epitomises a celebration of the superficial, the 'now' and the 'me'. Because it all moves so quickly, nothing appears important especially as the solid connections of family, authority, structure and morality have mostly been eroded. Therefore many of us have a problem with giving 'deep' commitment as we may have done in the past, because now if you fully commit to a cause or movement, it will have gone out of fashion or be overtaken by something else very quickly. Even the mainstream religions are giving way, not to other forms of belief, but to no beliefs at all.

We all understand the bigger macro-environmental messages such as global warming and poverty, but we are generally cynical that the actions of the individual can really make a difference. That's why so many people don't bother to vote. This is a result of the consumer power and recognition we hold, after all if we are fêted as individuals by advertising, publicity and the big brands, how can we believe that our actions have global or collective consequences? It's not so much a post-modernist culture as post post-modernist.

So whilst hierarchical structures have broken down, big issues are commoditised, consumer power is king and customers are seduced by the 'here' and the 'me', believing you have unquestionable customer loyalty is commercial suicide. When conducting business always act as if your existing customers are new ones, and never take them for granted.

Evaluate marketing activity by its return on investment

Marketing must move away from its current perception by other professions as a fluffy activity involving brainstorms, PR luvvies and the fuzzy art of gaining attention and measuring 'recall' as the one and only success criteria. It will never be taken seriously until Managing Directors, Finance Directors, HR Directors and the like, view it as an investment and not a cost. Clients must, and given the economy, will, become more insistent on evidence of tangible return on marketing spend. What sane client is happy paying for campaigns that top the weekly *Marketing* magazine table for recall by consumers, but don't measure anything you can put your finger on? Shouldn't the industry be celebrating marketing's contribution to incremental sales, not whether some person interviewed in Stevenage High Street remembered that advert on the tv last night? The same can be said of the public sector. Charity communications only really count if there are more donations than before it started. A government health campaign only matters if the target audience change and stop, or modify, their 'at risk' behaviour. A smoking cessation programme is only successful if people give up, not if they're thinking about it, or recognise the advert or can articulate the evidence that it's bad for them.

But that is just the beginning. Whilst the importance of financial returns is a key measure in the private sector, it isn't the only one. It just tells you what happened last month. It doesn't give clues for next month's performance, or next year's. If marketing takes centre stage in the business, becomes a philosophy not a process, and as articulated in my definition you agree it is *"about gaining and keeping a positive, word of mouth reputation."* The measure that keeps your finger on the pulse, that tells you whether your business will continue to thrive, is (not surprisingly) your word of mouth reputation. If your customers aren't as impressed by your company as they used to be, if they can find the same elsewhere but cheaper or if customer service quality is waning, you want to know about it. That way you can put in place corrective actions.

Hard, tangible return on investment measures will help you evaluate the current efficacy of your marketing operation. Tracking your word of mouth reputation will help secure the future of your business.

Recognise customer power

All the above key themes are likely to rise to prominence in the next few years, and add up to an increase in customer power whichever way you look at it. Whether that customer is a member of the community you serve, a business client or a shopper, you and your business are entirely dependent on them, so recognise it and treat them accordingly.

They may act individually but they can quickly organise themselves into groups if they have to. They can make their own music (audio editing), movies (web video), radio shows (podcasts), art galleries (online exhibition promotion sites) and magazines (blogs). They can instantly become producers, editors, publishers, content developers, promoters, distributors, re-mixers, up loaders and down loaders. In fact, they can do all the things that used to be in the hands of 'the establishment'.

In general, they wield their power lightly and quietly, but don't ever underestimate them because of it. If you really hack them off, they have the ability to destroy you.

INDEX